LUCKY PEACH

A QUARTERLY JOURNAL OF FOOD AND WRITING

Peter Meehan
EDITORIAL DIRECTOR

Chris Ying
EDITOR-IN-CHIEF

David Chang
EDITOR

Rachel Khong
EXECUTIVE EDITOR

Rupa Bhattacharya
SENIOR EDITOR

Devin Washburn
ART DIRECTOR

Joanna Sciarrino
MANAGING EDITOR

Ryan Healey
WEB EDITOR

Aralyn Beaumont
RESEARCH EDITOR

Rob Engvall
JUNIOR DESIGNER

Emily Johnson
EDITORIAL ASSISTANT

Brette Warshaw
CHIEF OPERATING OFFICER

Peter Romero
ACCOUNT EXECUTIVE

Nikkie Bertrand
EVENTS & OPERATIONS
ASSOCIATE

Rachele Morino
CIRCULATION SPECIALIST

CONTRIBUTORS:

Gabriele Stabile
ITALIAN PHOTOGRAPHER

Mark Ibold
SE PENNSYLVANIA
CORRESPONDENT

SPECIAL THANKS TO

Sascha Bos, Charlotte Goddu, Lauren Leibowitz, C.B. Owens, Pat Sims, Lucas Turner, Mary Jane Weedman, Nicole Wong, Eliza Wright

HELPING HANDS

Candy Argondizza, JJ Basil, Tina Battock, Florence Cane, Chris Chen, Caroline Cohen, Kristin Cunningham, Michelle Curb, Mitchell Davis, Glossmarc, Jonathan Gold, Brooks Headley, Eli Horowitz, Kateryna at Hired Hands Models, Stephen Kent, Christopher Kostow, Marie-Aude Laurent, Pat Nourse, Daniel Patterson, Jasmine Peterlin, Andrea Petrini, Jason Polan, Katerina Rakova, Sara Salaway, Marya Spence, Christina Tosi, Laurie Woolever

READ MORE AND SUBSCRIBE AT

LUCKYPEACH.COM

ALWAYS UPDATED AND UP-TO-DATE
MADE OUT OF PIXELS INSTEAD OF PAPER

Letters, submissions, *mignardises,* etc. will find us at either of the below addresses:

128 Lafayette Street,
Suite 302,
New York, NY 10013

12 Geary Street,
Suite 207,
San Francisco, CA 94108

Lucky Peach (USPS 12438) (ISSN 2325-9140) is published quarterly in Spring, Summer, Fall, and Winter by Lucky Peach LLC, 128 Lafayette St., Suite 302, New York, NY 10013. Periodicals postage paid at New York, NY and additional mailing offices. POSTMASTER: Send address changes to Lucky Peach, PO Box 433324 Palm Coast, FL 32143-9559. CanadaPost customer number 42740020.

Printed by RR Donnelley
in Liberty, MO

Logotype above by Daniel Clowes

Original Lucky Peach logotype by Brian McMullen

The display typeface used throughout this issue, Frauen, was designed by Lucas Sharp.

Have you ever Snapchatted?
Wanna Snapchat with us?
Scan this code and let's be friends ;)

ADVERTISING INQUIRIES: ADS@LKY.PH
PRESS INQUIRIES: PRESS@LKY.PH
CUSTOMER SERVICE: 877-292-1504
OR 386-246-0565 (OUTSIDE THE U.S.)

COVER ART BY
Aleksandra Kingo
OPENING PAGE ART
Pablo Delcan

BALLOON ART BY
Rob Driscoll
COVER TYPOGRAPHY
Braulio Amado

TASTE IS THE TRUE TEST.
BRIGHT CITRUS AROMAS AND A BOLD HOP FINISH MAKE GOOSE IPA THE CHOICE FOR BEER JUDGES AND BEER LOVERS ALIKE. BECAUSE TASTE IS THE TRUE TEST.
GOOSE IPA
Bright citrus aromas ★ BOLD HOP FINISH
TO WHAT'S NEXT. GOOSEISLAND.COM
GOOSE ISLAND BEER CO.
©2016 Goose Island Beer Co., Goose IPA®, India Pale Ale, Chicago, IL | Enjoy responsibly.

In This Issue

Editor's

ello, welcome to our third Cooks & Chefs outing. Please, can we take your coat? Here, have this glass of champagne on the house—this is the Fine Dining Issue, after all.

Now that you're settled in, may I tell you that I can't count the number of times I've been given the fine-dining-is-dead speech by David Chang, who has a pugilistic essay to that effect on page 38? (I will note, not incidentally, that he has his own F-word D-word restaurants in New York, Toronto, and Sydney.)

Me? I tend to hit the snooze button when the internecine battles of the food world flare up like toddlers with soiled diapers. So maybe the thing that pushed this issue into motion was the Will Guidara effect. I was recently

chatting with Guidara, the impresario and restaurateur behind Eleven Madison Park and its related property, the NoMad, and he was on the fine-dining-is-great-and-necessary trip. The guy could sell a time-share in an oceanfront condo to a mother sea turtle digging a nest on the beach it'd be built on. All in all, it feels like a time when things are changing: the World's 50 Best Restaurants lists have helped internationalize the face of "fine dining" (even if they've kept it fairly white and male); fine dining restaurants have been radically casualized over the past fifteen to twenty years; and food has moved from an oddball interest of the plump and moneyed to a central fixture in popular entertainment and culture.

So a who/what/where/when

approach seemed like a good place to start unscrambling the egg of where fine dining is today. We've assembled a few tools to help you (and us!) get your bearings. There's an illustrated portfolio of thirty iconic dishes that are part of the lingua franca of fancy restaurants on page 96, and a timeline on page 31: mile markers along the road from eating with our hands to eating off plateware specially designed by a chef for a particular amuse-bouche. We learn that chefs clucking like the sky is falling isn't particularly new. One excised example: in 1971, Roger Fessaguet, executive chef at La Caravelle (a dearly departed and very lovely New York restaurant), cautioned that the more inclusive immigration laws of 1965 would extinguish "haute cuisine in this country within s Note

a decade." Looking back, you could argue that haute cuisine had barely been practiced in America in 1971. In forty-five years, what will we make of 2016? My guess is that the sky stays in its place.

What we've done between these covers is try to answer the questions of what fine dining is, where it's going, and why it matters to people who participate in its propagation. I spent time with Iliana Regan, a chef in Chicago who is working at a high level on a limited budget in a small space. Tienlon Ho documented the work of chef Corey Lee and his ambitious new project at the San Francisco Museum of Modern Art. Brooks Headley and Wes Avila talk about why they left fine dining behind on pages 124 and 126. Anthony Bourdain, the reason why so

many of us care about restaurants at all, introduces an excerpt of George Orwell's *Down and Out in Paris and London*, and explains why it was and is important to him.

It had been a long time since I'd personally done any exploration into newer "fine dining" food, but during the making of this issue I had a chance to eat at Blanca, Carlo Mirarchi's fancy spot hidden behind Roberta's in Brooklyn. I found him making riotously flavorful food that was new and cool and fun to eat. I attended a lunch thrown by Andrea Petrini's nebulous Gelinaz! organization, where Enrico Crippa, a chef with three Michelin stars in Piedmont, Italy, combined forces with Jeremiah Stone and Fabián von Hauske Valtierra at their restaurant Contra, on New York's

Lower East Side. There was a course of cherries and shrimp and flowers in a cherry broth that literally stopped the day, stopped time, that was so arrestingly beautiful and inexplicably delicious that everything seemed better, possibilities felt endless.

With some frequency, we at *Lucky Peach* have the opportunity to cross paths with the people who dedicate themselves to the cooking profession at its highest level. They're often thoughtful and caring, and we're excited to have so many of them together in this issue. So even if your idea of a great dinner out is an extra Doritos Locos Taco when you drive through the local Taco Bell, hear out the folks in this issue—plenty of whom do the same thing, too.

—Peter Meehan

This Issue's Menu

Fancy Sauce
by Jim Meehan

Avenue
Passion fruit sorbet, lemon, and bourbon
Adapted from the
CAFÉ ROYAL COCKTAIL BOOK
22

Three Dishes: Chicken
by Sam Henderson

Roast Chicken
Whole roast chicken with soy-agave glaze
for weeknight dinners
136

Fried Chicken
Hawaiian style with Spam fried rice
for staff meals and other gatherings
139

Chicken Sausage
Boudin blanc with mustard,
potato noodles, and broccoli crumbs
for a fine dining restaurant
140

nature need
not be a STRANGER

Before our lives were so convenient, they were authentic.
We woke with the sun, worked with our hands and slept under the stars.
That may not be where we live anymore,
but it's a nice place to visit.
Get the guide at Colorado.com

COME TO LIFE COLORADO

The Lucky Peach Atlas

by Sean Brock

Illustrations by Paige Mehrer

Since the rest of the issue is stuffed with ortolans stuffed with foie gras stuffed with truffles stuffed into partridges, here is a palate cleanser of hoity-toity cuisine's spiritual foil: soul food. These are chef Sean Brock's picks for Michelin star-free eating in Charleston, South Carolina, where he's spent most of the past decade spreading the gospel of Southern food at his restaurants Husk and McCrady's (and slinging excellent tacos at his taqueria, Minero).

Bowens Island Restaurant
1870 Bowens Island Road
Charleston, South Carolina

Eating at Bowens Island is an amazing way to experience Charleston: you get to watch guys bring the oysters in, rinse them off, and cook them over an open fire. It's an old standby. It's been there forever and ever, though it burns down every few years and they have to rebuild it!

The guy who goes out every morning, Goat, is the same guy who's been plucking oysters there since he was nine—he's probably seventy or eighty now. They take a snow shovel, shovel the oysters onto the open fire, and toss a wet burlap sack over them. You're sitting at a table with a hole in the middle over a huge trash can for shells, and there's just *decades* of graffiti everywhere. They give you shuckers, towels, and this really watery, delicious cocktail sauce, and bring the wood-fire-roasted oysters by the cluster with the shovel and dump them on the table. It's like an all-you-can-eat situation, but you can't ask for more until you've cleaned the table. For those who've had their fill of oysters, they do an amazing classic Low Country boil there, too.

Category: Time Warp
What to order: roasted oysters; Low Country boil

Nana's Seafood and Soul
176 Line Street
Charleston, South Carolina

This place has like three tables, and serves a dish that doesn't get any action on most Charleston menus: garlic crabs—steamed or boiled crabs swimming in a garlic-herb butter. As you're picking through the crab, all that butter and herb and garlic gets all over your fingers, and your fingers basically flavor the meat as you eat. They also do fried crabs: they actually bread the entire live crab and fry it. They serve it with the garlic-herb butter, so again, as you're cracking the crab, your fingers get covered in butter and all that breading, which you eat with the super moist crab meat as you're picking through.

If you're lucky, they'll have crab rice or shrimp rice on the daily specials menu. They also do okra soup, fried whiting—the classics. These are the things that people cook in their homes around here—old, old Gullah/Geechee traditions. They do stewed cabbage that's dark brown, it's got so much crazy flavor. I like their deviled crabs a lot—a stuffed crab where you've picked out all the meat, mixed it with bread crumbs, onions, celery, and Old Bay–style spices, whatever you want to use, and then stuffed it back into the crab. That's another Low Country dish that hasn't seen its glory days yet. Nana's is one of the few restaurants in town that serves a really good version of it. They post all these great photos on Instagram, and refer to their telephone number as the "crabline bling." Nana's adds so much to the city. It's crazy, crazy good, and so cheap it's almost free.

Category: Safe Haven
What to order: garlic crabs; fried crabs; deviled crabs; stewed cabbage

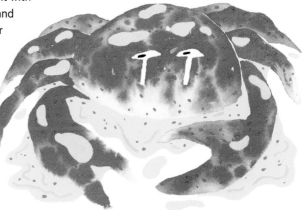

Hannibal's Kitchen
16 Blake Street
Charleston, South Carolina

Hannibal's is the kind of restaurant that inspires me: it hasn't changed in forty years and serves insanely delicious food. It's a soul food restaurant behind the old Johnson & Wales University, where I went to culinary school. My favorite thing to eat there is crab rice—buttered rice topped with crab that's been pan-fried with bell pepper, celery, onion, and bacon. It's a very important Gullah/Geechee dish that is most often consumed at home for special occasions, because it takes a *lot* of crab. At Hannibal's it's like seven bucks—it feels so wrong to pay so little but it tastes so good, I can't stop myself. I used to go there all the time when I was in school. As a student it's one of the most decadent and luxurious things you could ever eat while you're killing time between classes. Plus, it's the only soul food restaurant that I've ever been to where you can sit at the bar and have a beer.

Category: Specialists
What to order: crab rice and beer

Martha Lou's Kitchen
1068 Morrison Drive
Charleston, South Carolina

I stand by Martha Lou's, because the lima beans there haunt me. I just have to have them. They're a perfect example of the power, craft, and art of soul food: taking something so humble and so inexpensive, and applying your skill and wisdom to create something that's as luxurious as white truffles. You're probably thinking to yourself, *There's no way those lima beans are that good.* But put them in your mouth, and you won't believe what's going on. It's the most comforting and flavorful thing you could ever imagine. Those are the kind of dishes I love. That's what I like to eat best at Martha Lou's—I'll sometimes just go for a to-go container of them—though of course the fried chicken's amazing. That's a no-brainer.

Category: Safe Haven
What to order: lima beans; fried chicken

The Glass Onion
1219 Savannah Highway
Charleston, South Carolina

The Glass Onion is on the outskirts of town and doesn't get the recognition it deserves. It's been around for a while, and has young, enthusiastic owners that are well trained and cooking really simple, honest food, prepared masterfully. If I'm away from Charleston for a week or so, it's usually the first place I go when I get back; it's maybe the place my mom and I visit together the most. It's almost not a restaurant; it's counter service and super laid-back with extremely comforting Low Country food. I go and sit down and order a bowl of shrimp and grits. They slice the shrimp in half and cook them gently. I love how comforting and simple it is.

Category: Simple Pleasures
What to order: shrimp and grits **LP**

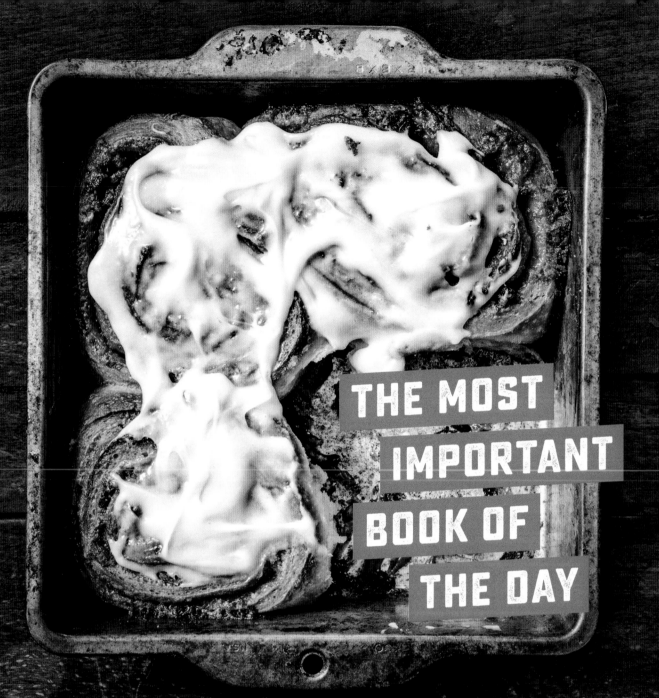

THE MOST IMPORTANT BOOK OF THE DAY

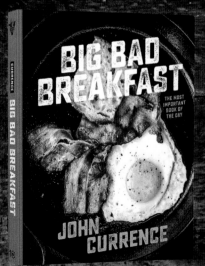

Classic Butter Taste

BY Walter Green

L ike many of you (I assume, no offense), I am a fully grown adult who lives with roommates. The epicenter of a household like ours is the kitchen. In our home, we generally share our food, especially if one of us gets a surplus of something.

When this magazine told me that for my next assignment I'd be receiving twenty-three packages of fancy butter, I couldn't help but feel like a capital-G, capital-R Good Roommate. More than a good roommate, actually. I felt like a rapper who had struggled for years, finally made it big, and then let all the people who had stood by him join in on his new lavish lifestyle. Since there are so many ways to use butter (on toast, in baking, in a pan, on veggies, in sauces, as a terrible thing to put in your

coffee, etc.), I also felt like a hunter-gatherer who'd brought enough dead animal carcasses back to the cave to last his tribe for two winters.

The only catch was that before any of this butter could enter into our kitchen ecosphere, I'd have to taste-test it. I should summarize the conditions of the test itself. Please read this very quickly, like the side effects at the end of a TV drug advertisement: the initial taste test was conducted over the course of two days via a spoonful (or spoonfuls) of each butter, with no bread, crackers, or accompaniment of any kind. I attempted (with varying success) to ignore the text on the butter until after the test was completed. Additional testing was done intermittently on toasted white bread.

Kerrygold Pure Irish Butter (Ireland)

This feels like a good starting butter. The shiny gold packaging communicates fanciness, a design trope I'll see again and again over the course of this tasting. Also, like many of the other butters, Kerrygold extols the conditions that their cows are kept in, specifically the lush Irish grass that the cows feed on all day. While Irish butter is not as romantic as butter from, say, France or Italy, it's still from Europe, so I'm still turned on a little! ;) The color is not the deepest yellow but not the lightest, either. It tastes like extremely good butter tastes. It kind of creeps up on you and builds like a rich, creamy crescendo as it melts in your mouth. Someone arrest me for what I just typed.

Organic Spring Hill Jersey Butter
European Style (California)

At first I'm like, *Man, all-American Jersey butter? That's what I'm talking about!* This is the type of butter you eat when you're blasting some Bruce in your muscle car on your way to work at the factory. But it turns out that Jersey is a breed of cow, originally from Jersey, a small "bailiwick" that is a part of the Channel Islands, between England and France. Bruce would never be caught dead in a bailiwick! It tastes a lot like butter. It's more mild than the last one. But still buttery. I don't exactly know how to write this article.

Somerdale English Country Butter (England)

More gold packaging, more language about cows grazing in lush pastures. One thing I should note: a lot of reviews of this butter noted that it was specifically "better than Kerrygold." To me, it's not. It has comparable richness (which is to say, very rich), but it's a bit sharper, almost like cheese. I make a note to myself: *Is cheese butter?*

Les Prés Salés Butter (Belgium)

The packaging is tasteful—a red-and-blue design printed on thin parchment paper. There's an illustration of a boy piling up salt from the sea. Is that the secret behind this butter? A small boy in an odd hat gathers all the salt? The butter itself is a bit sweaty. The color is spotty, with darker bits of yellow. The salt is large and visible and really makes its presence known. I'm hit by a quick rush of saltiness that lingers, followed by a wave of sweetness.

Haverton Hill Creamery Sheep Butter (California)

This butter is the color of lemon sorbet. The texture is markedly different from the butters thus far, not as smooth, less easily spreadable, and much more likely to break apart as you try to slice it. There's something slightly off about the flavor, almost a sour note. It might be that it spoiled while en route to my house, but I'm more inclined to believe that sheep just produce sour-tasting butter. Some farming message boards reveal that sheep's milk is often higher in fat and that sheep are more difficult to get milk from. My solution? Let's stop milking sheep!!!! Just kidding.

Sierra Nevada Cheese Company
European Style Vat-Cultured Butter (California)
The packaging is silver, so you already know it's less fancy. They claim to have no more than three cows per acre, that those cows roam the pastures for more than three hundred days a year, and that they observe sustainable farming practices such as "rotational grazing." I make another note to myself: *Rotational grazing? Do they put the cow on a big ol' spinning bed??? Lol.* This one is light in color and has a pretty mellow flavor.

Red Feather Brand Pure Creamery Butter (New Zealand)
This butter comes in a can! It's a very deep yellow, very creamy butter. It's not among the best, but the customers on Amazon have some pretty interesting uses for it. Many buy it and add it to their disaster-preparedness kits. One guy, who I'm slightly concerned for, says, "I keep BROWN BREAD IN A CAN for emergencies, pop open a can, spread some butter and you have a meal." Another customer bought some for her son-in-law who was stationed in Afghanistan, and some other guy says he bought a case for the "long haul"! I imagine this guy driving across the United States chowing down on butter.

H. J. Wijsman Provision Merchant
Preserved Dutch Butter (The Netherlands)
Another can. In my mind, because they are in sturdier packaging, canned butters should be more valuable. But in truth, they're probably designed for people who live in bunkers and don't care what they eat as long as they can eat it forever. I'm a bit disappointed in the taste (of both cans so far, actually). One positive thing: the color is a beautiful golden yellow, probably the most beautiful butter yet. But then I see they use beta-carotene as a food coloring. How dare you try to pull one over on me, can of butter!?

Beurdell Finest Quality Butter (France)
The packaging of this canned butter from France evokes a cat food marketed exclusively to depressed or bored cats. I don't have high hopes, although I am pleasantly surprised after popping the top to find that there's a sort of crown-shaped mound of butter right in the center. It's the least-sweet butter I've had so far, comparable to a sharp spreadable cheese in terms of taste and consistency. Cans of butter aren't good.

Beurre de Chimay (Belgium)
I'm actually quite psyched to eat another classic butter after the cans debacle. It reminds me of happier times when I was eating Kerrygold. The taste doesn't disappoint—this is another extremely rich, sweet, and creamy butter. My roommate Camryn loves it. When another roommate comes home, I take it as an excuse to end day one of butter testing. Later, I look in the mirror and find butter in my beard. Later still, I find butter on my glasses somehow. I shower and go to bed. The smell of butter lingers on my hands.

Beurre d'Échiré (France)

Man, this is a straight-up delicious butter. It also comes in probably the most "fine dining" packaging: a cute little basket. It's renowned for its high butterfat content—84 percent! (The average for most American butters is 81 percent.) As I understand it, more fat means less moisture, which makes for a better cooking butter, as it melts more evenly. *Lucky Peach* accidentally sent me two of these butters, which is lucky for me: 85 percent of all Échiré butter stays in France.

Plugrá European Style Salted Butter
(America—couldn't find a more specific origin!)

When I told people that I'd be doing a butter tasting, I was surprised by the number of people who asked if I'd be tasting Plugrá. (The number is two, so I guess I am easily surprised.) Plugrá is the American answer to European high-fat butters. At 82 percent butterfat, it's above the standard American amount but not quite at Échiré levels. It tastes really salty and good. The flavors rise and plateau together as the butter melts, similar to Kerrygold.

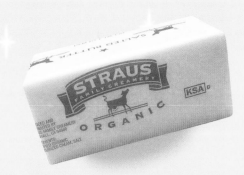

Straus Family Creamery European-Style Organic Salted Butter (California)

Wait, wait, wait. Forget everything I just said. This butter has 85 percent butterfat! That's way more than Plugrá. Apparently, though, this product is available less widely than the Ploog, but it's still used by chefs, especially Bay Area chefs like Alice Waters. I even read that Alice was the one who convinced them to start using such high amounts of fat. The flavor is deep and salty, and leaves a bit of a nutty aftertaste.

Miyoko's Creamery European Style Cultured Vegan Butter (California)

I'm pretty excited for this one, because it's so different from the rest. The ingredients are organic coconut oil, water, organic safflower oil or organic sunflower oil, organic cashews, soy lecithin, sea salt, and cultures. The butter is so white. Have you seen the movie *Powder* about the really pale guy? This butter is the *Powder* of butter. The taste is okay, a passing substitute for cow butter. It's got a slight tang and bitterness. I can imagine a dystopian future where there is no butter and we have to eat this stuff, and it's okay. Or I can just imagine eating it in the regular present day if you are a vegan person.

Double Devon Cream Butter (England)

The best thing about this butter is its shape, like a large Tootsie Roll made of butter. It's the size of an organic frozen burrito, and I even unwrap it like I would a burrito. I decide to forgo a knife and just bite it. I take several bites, actually, and stare out my window, hoping someone will see me, a grown man chomping down on a burrito of butter. This one's pretty good—another creamy, classic butter taste. I make a note to myself: *How many times will I say "classic butter taste"?*

Meggle Alpenbutter (Germany)

I'm pretty tired of gold packaging, but I will say that this has a light and refreshing taste. I mean this in a good way: it's almost got a toothpaste-like sensation. It hits an area and sort of quickly spreads coolness in that area. It's a good palate cleanser. I eat four scoops to try to figure out more things to say about this butter. Hey, crazy coincidence, my first girlfriend and the love of my life was named Meggle Alpenbutter.

Delitia Butter of Parma (Italy)

Finally, a butter where the packaging actually feels high quality to me, not just an approximation of what people will think is fancy. It's wrapped in a slightly coarse paper with a subtle throwback design. When I open it up, I feel that I am a young, beautiful Italian boy in the fifties whose mother sent him out to buy the best butter at a local market. Their packaging says that their milk is "strictly selected in accordance with extraordinary and rigorous disciplinary of production." The fact that that makes no sense only endears this butter more to me.

Fond O' Foods German Butter (Germany)

This butter looks like trash. The illustrations of a cow and grass look like they were done by a Fond O' Foods intern who didn't know the Adobe Creative Cloud applications but lied on their resumé and said they were well versed in design, so they had to really quickly figure out how to use Illustrator. The only thing I like about this butter is the name Fond O' Foods. If you work for Fond O' Foods and you're reading this, please connect with me on LinkedIn and we can discuss opportunities in rebranding and merchandising.

Lurpak Imported Butter (Denmark)

I really enjoy pronouncing this butter's name. *Lerrr-pahk.* Say it with me. *Lerrr-pahk.* It sounds like the name of a corporate conglomerate that has a very friendly public persona but is extremely shady behind the scenes. Sound off in the comments below if you know what Lurpak means. It sort of tastes the way our refrigerator smells, and could use some salt.

Clover Organic Farms Salted Butter (California)
This butter tastes even more like our refrigerator. My roommate Rachel theorizes that it's because it's wrapped in wax paper and thus more susceptible to the flavors of its environment. Whatever, Poindexter! This butter comes from "a select group of family farms on the North Coast of California." If I were a farmer, it would be my lifelong dream to join this gang of elite farmers. I would join, then I would be excited for a couple weeks, and then I would get tired of that and realize I'll never really be fulfilled. Anyway, I really enjoyed this butter.

Landliebe Butter (Germany)
I don't want to start drama in the butter community, but I think the design of this butter is a rip off of Meggle Alpenbutter. Landliebe is another butter that is close in texture/spreadability to cream cheese. It's probably getting the short end of the stick, because I am so tired of tasting butter. Some anagrams of Landliebe: lendable, deniable, edible LAN.

Grand Cru Lescure Beurre Charentes-Poitou (France)
I guess it's a pretty good problem to have, to be tired of eating butter. But I really am so sick of chewing butter. It feels unnatural and, frankly, dark. This butter retains its shape pretty well when you slice it, and it has a velvety mouthfeel. It's good, but not one of the best. If you're a kid trying to decide which butter you want to be when you grow up, it's fine if you end up like this one, but you should probably aim for a better one. I'm starting to feel unclean, like butter is spreading over my lips and filling up the pores on my face.

St Helen's Farm Goats' Butter (England)
I recently watched a horror film, *The Witch*, where (SPOILER ALERT) the Devil takes the form of a goat named Black Phillip. He proposes a trade for a young woman's eternal servitude, slowly and sensually whispering, "Wouldst thou like the taste of butter?... Wouldst thou like to live deliciously?" So it's fitting that I end on the butter of a goat. Upon tasting, I make my last note: *It tastes like lamb, like a lamb that got turned into butter. Cream of lamb. Does goat taste like lamb?* I've never tasted goat. If this is the butter that the Devil is offering, I don't think he will get many takers. I might recommend that he opt for a more classic butter taste.

With the tasting done, I feel a weight lift from my shoulders. My apartment's era of fine dining can finally begin. LP

Fancy Sauce

Raising the bar with Micah Melton

BY JIM MEEHAN

The role of the bar in fine dining restaurants has changed dramatically since I took my first restaurant gig in New York City in 2002. Back then, the bar functioned as a waiting room for the main event in the dining room. Today, most fine dining restaurants offer their full menu at the bar and include cocktails as part of the dining experience.

The groundwork for this sea change was laid in the late nineties and early aughts, when the cocktail returned to its roots after a decades-long incarnation as a vodka-delivery vehicle. A handful of precocious "bar chefs" started mixing cocktails with the same ingredients and earnestness as their counterparts in the kitchen. Thanks to seasonal, market-minded bartenders like Nick Mautone at Danny Meyer's Gramercy Tavern, Eben Freeman at Wylie Dufresne's wd~50, and Thad Vogler at Charles Phan's the Slanted Door, the craft of bartending was revived and thrives in as many restaurants as bars today.

Thanks to bar-championing chefs like Paul Kahan (the Violet Hour), Barbara Lynch (Drink), Linton Hopkins (Holeman and Finch), and Daniel Humm (the NoMad Bar), more and more bartenders are taking cues from the rigorous work ethic, high standards, professionalism, mastery of flavor, ingredients, and technique of the kitchen.

Few have had a better perch to witness the transformation than Micah Melton, who trained in Grant Achatz's kitchen before opening his cocktail bar, the Aviary, in 2011. He now oversees the entire restaurant group's cocktail program. I asked him about what he's learned along the way and where he thinks cocktail culture is headed.

JIM MEEHAN: You worked with Craig Schoettler (the iconoclastic chef who opened the Aviary in 2011) and Charles Joly (the legendary bartender who took it over in 2012) before taking the reins. How have their styles and approaches influenced yours? How would you characterize your style?

MICAH MELTON: Schoettler taught me that anything is possible. Multisensory crazy presentation can work if you prepare and organize yourself before the guest walks in. Charles taught me how to make drinks for people—refining my palate and making sure I was putting things on the menu that people wanted to drink and were balanced for them, and not necessarily me. Also, in some cases, that less is more. If a three-ingredient drink with a flavorful ice cube was spot-on, why add four more things?

I would say my style is a marriage of those things. Obviously presentation has a huge part in our drinks, but it never detracts from the flavor of the cocktail—it should only add layers of complexity and give people another memorable element.

JM: Eleven Madison Park was the first four-star restaurant in New York that really embraced cocktails, and now you'll find them in many more places, although most probably don't do much with them. Will this change?

MM: I think we have yet to see fine dining restaurants fully embrace cocktail programs. I would love to see them focus their discipline, standards, and organization toward cocktails, however.

JM: What does "fine dining" mean to you from a cocktail perspective?

MM: Well, here at the Aviary I think it is all about service.

If you order a drink and get up to use the restroom or make a phone call, we will stop making your drink until you return. We don't want to drop a drink and have you enjoy it past its prime.

Descriptions and knowledge have a huge impact as well. Our team spends countless hours learning the intricacies of all the components of our drinks so you can ask anything about a cocktail or dish and the servers will know it.

For us at the Aviary, it's also important that we offer only what's on our menu. We work many hours

on cocktails before they make our menu, and we have about twenty to twenty-five at any given time. We don't make drinks that aren't on that menu for the same reason the French Laundry doesn't make you an off-menu hamburger. Could they make it amazing? Of course. Is it as ironed out, organized, and honed as the offerings on the menu? No chance.

JM: A lot of bartenders and chefs brag about drinking shitty beer and shots when they're off work, but you don't see somms drinking Franzia on their nights off. What about you? And how do you think this affects perceptions of "fancy" cocktail bars both in the trade and public?

MM: A lot of the time, after work you want to experience what you don't work with all the time. Does a cook at a Michelin-starred restaurant want to eat tasting menus on his day off, or grab a beer and a taco? I personally drink a lot of sour beer, Dark 'N Stormys, negronis, and chartreuse when I'm not at work. They're easy to make, easy to drink, and available most anywhere. There's something relaxing about having a go-to drink that you can get anywhere and not having a bad experience with a bad cocktail.

JM: Does your training in the front and back of the house make you a better bartender, or just a good fancy-restaurant bartender? What could bartenders who've never worked in fine dining learn and bring to their less-formal bars?

MM: The biggest thing I learned, honestly, is cleanliness. *Clean* glasses. I never spill, fingerprint, or overfill my glasses. Everything is thought out, so when the guest grabs their cocktail, it isn't overflowing, sticky, or wet—those are some of my biggest pet peeves. I also learned how to be elegant and quiet behind the bar. At some bars it's okay to bang things around, throw jiggers into empty sinks, and slam tins down. I like to think of my style as more refined and less of a distraction to my guests.

Avenue

Adapted from Micah Melton of the Aviary, this cocktail is an update of a recipe that originally appeared in the Café Royal Cocktail Book *in 1937*

Sorbet

8 oz passion fruit purée
2 oz lemon juice
4 oz simple syrup
2 oz apple brandy

Cocktail Base

$1\frac{1}{2}$ oz bourbon
1 oz water
$\frac{3}{4}$ oz lemon juice
$\frac{1}{2}$ oz simple syrup
$\frac{1}{4}$ oz grenadine

1. Make the sorbet: Combine the passion fruit purée (which you can get on Amazon from a company called Boiron), lemon juice, and simple syrup and freeze according to your ice cream maker's instructions. Transfer the spun sorbet to a pint container, freeze for at least a couple hours, then stir the apple brandy into the sorbet a few minutes before making the drink. This is enough sorbet for eight drinks, but it's hard to make less, plus who doesn't like extra sorbet laying around. Eat any excess with a spoon.

2. Put bubbles in the booze: Combine the cocktail base ingredients in a carbonating device (like a Pure-Fizz Soda Maker; making a batch in the slightly more common SodaStream is possible but requires you to carbonate a lot of cocktail fixins), and carbonate according to the manufacturer's instructions.

3. Scoop a quenelle of sorbet into a champagne flute and top with the cocktail base. **LP**

"IT DOESN'T MAKE YOU A BAD PERSON".

— Tito

So You Want To Open A Restaurant?

BY BOURREE LAM

Roughly 60 percent of independent restaurants go bust within three years. On average, a restaurant's operating costs eat up 90 to 95 percent of a restaurant's revenue. With margins like that, there's little room for mistakes.

Of course, there's a huge range when it comes to dining: fast food, fast-casual and mid-range dining, and high-end establishments. Still, the way that the basic costs break down for these different types of restaurants is similar (revenue comes from the food and beverages sold; expenses include raw materials, staff, and rent). It's the many nuances that end up making a big difference in their respective bottom lines.

Here, we're taking a look at the two ends of the spectrum—fast food and fine dining—to see how both sides make it work.

A NOTE ON METHODOLOGY:
The most solid data in the dining industry comes from the National Restaurant Association, which publishes key economic indicators on a monthly basis, as well as a yearly report that compiles financial information from a survey of more than 600 restaurants in the U.S. They offer a close look at balance sheet averages for restaurants of different check sizes. The numbers for fast-food chains, many of which are publicly listed, are also out in the open for investors and stockholders to scrutinize.

On the other hand, financial information for high-end restaurants, which make up less than 1 percent of the industry, has always been something of a mystery. The majority are privately owned, and the unpredictability of variable costs for high-end restaurants are especially volatile, meaning that for each individual restaurant, the costs and profit margins can be drastically different. The estimates and anecdotes in this article come from conversations with a dozen chefs, general managers, and restaurant owners, who gave us a picture of where their diners' dollars are going.

FINE DINING CONSIDERATIONS

FAST FOOD CONSIDERATIONS

START WITH A PILE OF MONEY

LABOR

Food and staffing costs are the largest expenses in operating any kind of restaurant. That's particularly true for fine dining establishments, where these fixed costs add up to nearly 70 percent of revenue. "Technically this is the figure, but a lot of fine dining restaurants struggle with that number," says Eric Ripert, chef and owner of Le Bernardin. "It makes it difficult to generate profits, which can explain why so many fine dining restaurant groups and chefs expand into different, more profitable concepts." Part of the labor cost at top restaurants is the investments that have gone into the skills of the staff. Fast-food workers—and most casual restaurant workers—are paid lower wages, and many chains have developed systems with the express purpose of lowering labor costs.

Michael Muser, general manager and partner at Grace in Chicago: "Any money that's made, massive chunks of it are going to labor. The employees outnumber the guests almost every night that I'm open."

Christopher Gaulke, lecturer in food and beverage management at Cornell University: "Fast casual and fast food invest initially in infrastructure: the facility, the equipment, the property plant, etc. They invest much larger numbers on average than a standard independent restaurant because it's all of the equipment and all of the systems they've developed that actually reduce that labor burden. Their labor costs might be a bit lower on a percentage basis because of that."

Mourad Lahlou, chef of Mourad in San Francisco: "It's hard to find good cooks who are willing to put in the energy and to cook at the level of a fine dining restaurant. For us, there's a portion of [labor costs] that's devoted to the cost of training. It takes weeks before they can get the chance to cook, but we want to invest in their skills."

FOOD AND BEVERAGE COSTS

The cost of raw ingredients accounts for somewhere between 30 and 35 percent of its revenue. Large restaurant chains are experts in sourcing and shipping food in large quantities to maximize efficiency. For example, a pizza chain can stabilize the cost of cheese by signing a yearlong contract with its suppliers. Independent restaurants that change menus nightly or weekly don't have that option. Shipping ingredients—seafood to a non-coastal fine dining restaurant, for example—can be a big concern. Finally, food waste is another cost that restaurant owners are acutely aware of.

Michael Muser: "Whatever's leftover [after labor], the chef will spend. Everything we're serving you costs a lot of money to buy, I promise."

Christopher Gaulke: "Where you'll see greater margins and greater consistency of margins are with the chain restaurants, because they've built in all of these different systems to mitigate those price risks. A large multi-unit chain is going to have price contracts for all of its major foods. You get different economies of scale."

Gene Tang, chef and owner of 1515 in Colorado: "Because fine dining restaurants use more expensive and exotic produce/protein, we need to watch our spending more than other restaurants. Our food is seasonal and very perishable, our waste is a bit higher."

Eric Ripert: "It's more difficult [with fine dining], because the operational costs can be higher, certain food items can't be produced at a large scale for more diners (say caviar versus potatoes)."

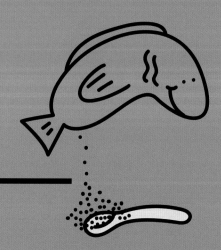

Jeff Katz, general manager at Del Posto in New York: "Depending where you are, in what city, your rent plays a big role. Depending on which region your restaurant is in; the cost of rent can really vary. Restaurants in big cities have the difficult task of balancing high rents if their owners don't own their space."

RENT

The cost of rent varies dramatically, and not just due to building size and geography. High-end restaurants with owners who supply a space might see lower costs of rent, but also pay out a larger cut of their profits. Rent for fast-food restaurants can be high due to a franchise's setup: McDonald's, for example, owns 70 percent of its buildings and 45 percent of the land. The company charges franchise owners as much as 16 percent of revenue in rent. Moreover, fast food restaurants often have to compete for expensive leases (in airports, for example) to get the foot traffic they need.

RAINY DAYS

The recession wasn't kind to restaurants in America. According to financial statement analysis of privately held restaurants, net profit margins were virtually nil during the recession as patrons cut back on eating out. But it's since bounced back, and as of 2013, profit margins have risen to an average of around 5 percent. Fine dining restaurants acutely feel fluctuations of the seasons and economy and how they affect diners' resources and inclination to spend a lot of money on dining. Last-minute cancellations and no-shows are also a huge problem at high-end restaurants. On any given night, empty seats eat into revenue. Given the high fixed costs, a financial cushion needs to be factored in.

Frank McClelland, executive chef and proprietor of L'Espalier in Boston: "A string of weekend blizzards can be catastrophic to the bottom line. In our nearly forty years in business, there has never been a big snowstorm on Valentine's Day. The thought of one is terrifying."

Joshua Skenes, chef of Saison in San Francisco: "One cancelled table can alter the financials by quite a bit. These productions are paid for in advance. We're already committed to buying X pounds of product or harvesting from our farms in labor, cost of goods. The restaurant has already paid for it. Once you understand both sides, cancellation really should be the full amount."

Jeff Elsworth, a restaurant industry expert and associate professor of hospitality business entrepreneurship at the Broad College of Business at Michigan State University: "Fine dining restaurants have to spend money to make money when it comes to atmosphere, labor, and food and beverage cost. They can, however, limit their expenses for things like marketing and administrative costs."

OTHER COSTS

In any restaurant, the money that's not going to raw materials, rent, and labor costs goes to repairs and maintenance, administration, marketing, insurance, worker's comp, cleanup, and other operating costs. At fine dining restaurants, additional resources are devoted to making dining a luxury experience. Bells and whistles—flowers, linens, china, glassware, candles, silver polish, uniforms—can each account for as much as 1 percent of revenue.

Jeff Elsworth: "Fast food restaurants can expect lower food and labor costs but need to spend more on marketing and, if it is a chain, administrative costs."

PROFIT!!!

Successful fine dining restaurants are built on fully booked dining rooms of customers willing to shell out for special occasions. Some restaurants also do a brisk private dining business, which is a boon for revenue. The highest-end restaurants can expect higher check-averages than virtually any other restaurant segment. In contrast, fast-food restaurants are built on volume. Profit comes from selling lots of food at lower prices and reaping the thin margins of a high number of transactions.

Those profits, if there are any, usually go into two pockets: the shareholders' or back to the restaurant as investments. In fine dining restaurants, money might also go to bonuses for chefs or managers, renovations, or R&D for inventing new techniques or dishes. **LP**

Mourad Lahlou: "Most people think of the relationship between expenditures of a restaurants and the quality of the experience and the food as a linear thing. If you pay more, you get more. It's really a tricky kind of situation where you can get from 0 to 90 percent perfect, but to get from 90 to 95 percent, you need to spend another 25 percent. You just get to the point where the curve is so steep that to make that incremental improvement, it takes so much."

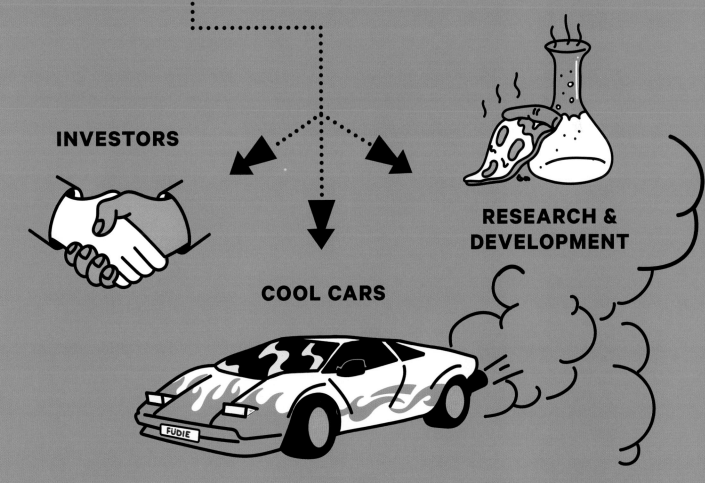

INVESTORS

COOL CARS

RESEARCH & DEVELOPMENT

CHEF'S SELECTION

crucible-fired cast iron and
seasonal accompaniments
Fresnoy-Le-Grand, France

LE CREUSET®

SAVOR LIFE

lecreuset.com

A Timeline of Fine Dining

BY **SASCHA BOS**

ILLUSTRATIONS BY **ROB ENGVALL**

I n literature, they talk about the canon—classic works, almost exclusively written by dead white guys. Those in favor of studying the canon will say that although these books may not reflect who we are now, we must continue reading them to understand their influence. TBH, I think, *Fuck that!* If we keep studying the same authors, we'll keep sounding like them. What if we just threw out the canon and started fresh?

But because food is a mentorship industry, big-name chefs influence the younger generation of chefs who train under them. And despite the fact that the story of fine dining is *not* made up entirely of French dudes, even the most forward-thinking chefs still espouse the virtues of a foundation in French cuisine.

Was it my heart's desire to turn a more or less blind eye to *kaiseki*, the complex history and recent rise of the American South, or what's happening in South America and Australia? No, but in piecing together the traditions that chefs and writers cite as the defining moments in fine dining, a pattern of people and events emerged, either because they presented something completely radical, embodied the culture of the time, or were just really good at self-promotion.

Being familiar with the mold can help us appreciate those who break it, and looking at fine dining as a timeline alerts us to the ways trends form (groundbreaking!) and fade (overdone). When a restaurant that doesn't quite fit the mold gains acceptance in the world of fine dining, that's worth noting. What happens in this relatively small corner of the food world can change the entire landscape. But at its most basic level, we hope this timeline will help orient you to the whos, whats, and whys of fine dining.

1547

Catherine de Medici becomes the Queen of France. With her arrival from Florence comes a coterie of cooks, chefs, winemakers, and gardeners, who have historically been credited with establishing the roots of high French cuisine. This apocryphal tale has been widely refuted, but the influence of Italian epicureanism on French dining is still a valid concept, and something you can lord over any French people you know.

Let's skip over the primordial ooze of fine dining and jump in again at the end of the eighteenth century:

Food service is controlled by guilds, the members of which (called *limonadiers* or *aubergistes* or *cafetiers*) are only licensed to sell a single product. In 1765, a Parisian shop owner named Boulanger tries to sell a dish of sheep's feet in white sauce in addition to his *restaurants* (fortifying soups). The guild of stew-makers sues him, and Boulanger wins. Shops selling multiple food items slowly appear around Paris. In 1789, French aristocrats and financiers flee their homes after the storming of the Bastille, "[throwing] all the good chefs out onto the pavement," according to Alexandre-Balthazar-Laurent Grimod de La Reynière. This rapidly accelerates the movement away from private kitchens; by the end of the French Revolution, Paris will be home to hundreds of restaurants.

1815

Marie Antonin Carême, who cooked for nobility across Europe and was famous for his fantastical sugar sculptures (*pièces montées*), publishes his first cookbooks, *Le pâtissier royal parisien* and *Le pâtissier pittoresque*. Carême's books (including *Le cuisinier parisien* and *L'Art de la cuisine française au XIXe siècle*) codify *grande cuisine*: he introduces the idea of separating meat, fish, and poultry; promotes the use of four mother sauces (*espagnole, velouté, allemande,* and *béchamel*); and classifies dishes and their variations along organizational trees.

1827

The Swiss Delmonico brothers open Delmonico's as a café in New York City. In 1830 it becomes, if not the first fine dining restaurant in America, the most influential of its time. Delmonico's focus on French cuisine—dishes like *consommé printanier, haricots verts*, and petit fours—set the standard for what Americans perceive as fine dining in the twentieth century.

1830s–1840

Boston's Tremont House brings Russian service (dishes are plated in the kitchen and served sequentially, one dish at a time) to America. Historically, restaurants have served in the French style, where a number of dishes are presented at once. In the 1860s, chef Félix Urbain-Dubois will popularize Russian service in France.

Antoine's, America's second high-end, non-hotel restaurant after Delmonico's, opens in New Orleans, serving French-Creole cuisine and setting a trend of regional fine dining in very slow motion.

As for the rest of the nineteenth century, historian Dr. Paul Freedman writes:

The mid-nineteenth century represents a distinctive phase in the history of American cuisine, one that lasted a long time, as culinary trends and fashions go. Indeed, until about 1890, less altered over the course of the century than one might expect... the dining experience of the Gilded Age was intimately tied to what had preceded it and, indeed, to traditions of American fine cuisine reaching back to the 1830s, at least.

1900

Michelin publishes its first guide, a free pamphlet for motorists with information on how to change a tire and locations of Michelin dealers and hotels. In 1923 they added a separate section for restaurant listings, and in 1926 they began awarding a star to outstanding restaurants. In 1931 a three-star system was introduced. The criteria, published in 1936, were: "one star: a very good restaurant in its category; two stars: excellent cooking, worth a detour; three stars: exceptional cuisine, worth a special journey."

1903

Auguste Escoffier publishes *Le Guide Culinaire*, which simplifies the ideas set forth by Carême and introduces the brigade system of organizing professional kitchens.

1933

Eugénie Brazier earns three stars for her restaurants La Mère Brazier in Lyon and Le Col de la Luère. She is the first chef to receive six Michelin stars.

Fernand Point receives his third Michelin star for his restaurant La Pyramide, in Vienne, near Lyon. In his kitchen begins the rumbles of what will later become a revolution in cuisine. Point was an early pioneer of ingredient-driven cuisine—changing his menu often to reflect quality and availability—and a mentor to Paul Bocuse, Jean and Pierre Troisgros, Alain Chapel, and Louis Outhier.

1939

The New York World's Fair opens in Flushing Meadows, Queens, with the theme "The World of Tomorrow." Participating countries create large "pavilions," complete with restaurants showcasing their national cuisines—like Epcot, without the cartoon mice. Marcel Olivier, French Commissioner General for the World's Fair, says, "American visitors are able to dine in New York in an atmosphere identical to that found in the restaurants of the Rue Royale or the Avenue de l'Opéra: same cuisine, same wine, same personnel, same charm." Despite being the most expensive dining option at the fair, Le Restaurant Français is overwhelmingly popular. Journalists complain about the difficulty of getting a table, although Le Restaurant is cited for violating capacity regulations by jamming twice as many seats into the space as permitted.

1941

Hoping to capitalize on the success of Le Restaurant Français, its former maître d' Henri Soulé opens Le Pavillon in Midtown East. In 1952, former Le Restaurant Français *premier commis poissonnier* Pierre Franey joins as executive chef. Jacques Pépin gets his first job in America at Le Pavillon in 1959. He remembers the famous *poulet Pavillon*: "A harmonious, rich, glistening roast chicken. We flavored the chicken simply with thyme, salt, and pepper and roasted it on high heat, basting regularly to give it a deep brown, crisp finish. Then we made a sauce of reduced chicken stock, Champagne, and cream, finishing it with cognac, and drizzled the reduced natural juices over the sauced bird." Le Pavillon alumni will go on to open New York's most famous French restaurants (including Le Mistral, La Grenouille, and La Côte Basque) under the same model: Escoffier-based haute cuisine served in a luxurious setting (white tablecloths, huge flower arrangements).

1942

The United States had entered World War II just before the start of the New Year. Restaurants cut back on sugar and coffee due to rationing, but more Americans start eating at restaurants, where they can pay for food with cash, rather than ration stamps. During the war, restaurants serve eight million meals a day (compared with three million before). French cuisine increases in popularity, while German food, once a respected fine dining option in New York City, loses its allure.

1957

Craig Claiborne becomes the next *New York Times* food critic, and edits the paper's food section for the next twenty-nine years. Claiborne will set the standard for restaurant reviews around the country, implementing a four-star rating system in 1964 and instituting a policy of three preferably anonymous visits. Claiborne awards his first four-star review to La Côte Basque in 1967. His candor and twenty-plus cookbooks open up haute cuisine to millions of readers.

1959

The Four Seasons opens in Manhattan, under the leadership of Joe Baum. It features a seasonal menu that's printed in English, both relatively new concepts in American fine dining.

1967

Brothers Michel and Albert Roux open landmark London restaurant Le Gavroche, serving grande cuisine and training what will eventually be the next generation of British culinary talent: Marco Pierre White, Gordon Ramsay, Pierre Koffmann, and Marcus Wareing.

1970

The term "celebrity chef" first appears in the *New York Times*, to describe Raymond Oliver, chef of Le Grand Véfour in Paris.

The early 1960s

Protégés of Fernand Point begin to pioneer *nouvelle cuisine*, a break from the strictures of Escoffier-style grande cuisine, marked by an emphasis on regional dishes, food plated in the kitchen, lighter sauces, and shorter cooking times.

At L'Auberge du Pont de Collonges, Paul Bocuse is in the first years of serving the wildly influential dishes that will define his legacy (and remain unchanged for decades): red mullet with potato scales, black-truffle soup VGE (named for French then-president Valéry Giscard d'Estaing), and Bresse chicken cooked inside a pig's bladder (*poularde de Bresse en vessie*, which he adopted from Point).

1971

Chez Panisse opens in Berkeley, California. The restaurant's hyper-seasonal, one-menu-a-night format is revolutionary in America. "It could probably only happen in Berkeley," begins the *San Francisco Examiner*'s earliest review. "Any experienced restaurateur could have set them straight in a few minutes as to why it would never work. But Berkeley being Berkeley, such sage advice wasn't sought—or, if it was, it was not heeded."

Meanwhile, Le Pavillon closes. Its progeny—La Caravelle, Lutèce, and La Grenouille—will all receive four-star ratings from the *New York Times* and survive the end of the century. Hunam, "the best Chinese restaurant in the city," becomes the first non-European restaurant to receive a four-star review from the *Times*.

1974

Michel Guérard develops *cuisine minceur*, an even lighter take on nouvelle cuisine: he subs a mixture of ricotta and yogurt for butter and thickens sauces with vegetable purées. As diners in the '70s grow more concerned about healthy living, cuisine minceur takes hold. Two years later, Guérard will begin serving cuisine minceur to New York's highest society at the exclusive club Regine's.

1978

Roger Vergé publishes *Ma cuisine du soleil*, promoting the style of Mediterranean-influenced nouvelle cuisine he cooks at his

restaurants on the southeastern coast of France, Le Moulin de Mougins and L'Amandier de Mougins. Chefs like Daniel Boulud, David Bouley, Alain Ducasse, and Hubert Keller all spend time in his kitchens.

Michel Bras begins serving *gargouillou* at his restaurant in Laguiole, France. The dish, of carefully arranged and minimally prepared vegetables, will spawn countless imitations throughout the 1990s and beyond.

1979

Times critic Mimi Sheraton correctly predicts that 1979 will see the emergence of nouvelle cuisine in America: in New York, the Quilted Giraffe and Dodin-Bouffant open, and Le Plaisir reinvents itself with a new name and two new chefs, one French and one Japanese. In Los Angeles, L'Orangerie begins to gain national recognition. In Santa Monica, Michael McCarty opens Michael's, tying modern French service to impeccable local ingredients and training a long list of chefs including Ken Frank, Jonathan Waxman, Mark Peel, Roy Yamaguchi, Sally Clarke, and Nancy Silverton.

Jean-Louis Palladin opens his first restaurant in America, Jean-Louis at the Watergate, leading the *Washingtonian* to dub him "the French chef who taught Washington how to eat." Palladin will mentor Eric Ripert, Daniel Boulud, and Sylvain Portay.

1981

Joël Robuchon takes over the kitchen at Jamin in Paris, where he will spend the decade defining the '80s approach to haute cuisine with his hyper-perfectionist nouvelle cuisine.

1982

Wolfgang Puck opens Spago in West Hollywood, after leaving the influential French restaurant Ma Maison. Puck introduces the world to the concept of the casual fine dining restaurant, and sensations like pizza topped with smoked salmon and caviar.

Chez Panisse alum Jonathan Waxman brings California cuisine to New York when he opens Jams on the Upper East Side. *New York Magazine* critic Gael Greene finds the "California relaxed elegance" of the dining room somewhat "undone" but admits that "those pricey California salads" with their "inevitable goat cheese... can be sublime." She calls California cooking "a translation of France's nouvelle cuisine." It will be a dominant mode of mid- to fine dining restaurants in America for decades to come.

1987

Nobuyuki Matsuhisa opens Matsuhisa in Beverly Hills, establishing the sushi bar as a part of the modern fine dining room.

In France, Ferran Adrià hears Jacques Maximin, chef at Le Chantecler, say, "Creativity means not copying," and decides to pursue an original identity in his cooking. In Chicago, Charlie Trotter opens his eponymous restaurant; national trends emerge from the chef's table (set and served in the kitchen), where Trotter will eventually showcase his vegetable tasting menus and, even later, his embrace of raw foods.

1990

Three years after opening, David Bouley's restaurant Bouley receives a four-star review from *New York Times* critic Bryan Miller. Miller says the chef's "rabid zeal for fresh regional ingredients, his cerebral approach to textures and flavors, and his obvious delight in wowing customers make this one of the most exciting restaurants in New York City."

Alain Ducasse's Le Louis XV in Monaco is the first hotel restaurant to receive three Michelin stars.

1991

Gray Kunz opens Lespinasse in the St. Regis Hotel in New York, where he incorporates Asian techniques and ingredients into very opulent and otherwise classic fine dining. An impressive collection of chefs pass through his doors, including Andrew Carmellini, Floyd Cardoz, Corey Lee, Shane McBride, Fabrizio Salerni, Rocco DiSpirito, and Brian Bistrong.

The James Beard Foundation, founded five years earlier, hands out its first awards, finally giving American chefs a prize to covet. (Michelin will not land in America for another decade and a half.)

1993

Ruth Reichl pens the most famous restaurant review ever written, about Le Cirque in New York City. She documents extreme differences in treatment when she visits as an anonymous patron versus as a recognized food critic.

Daniel Boulud has recently left Le Cirque after six years to open his own restaurant, Daniel, which eventually usurps Le Cirque's two-decades-old position as the premier French restaurant for power dining in the city and also becomes a lightning rod for critics and guidebooks looking to make a Reichl-like statement about the treatment of patrons in fine dining. Boulud's kitchen is the training ground for many chefs, including Alex Lee, Dominique Ansel, Johnny Iuzzini, Michael Anthony, Jonathan Benno, Alex Guarnaschelli, and Riad Nasr.

1994

In Spain, Ferran Adrià's restaurant El Bulli forms a development squad, "a team devoted to creativity," and a style of cooking they'll refer to as "technique-concept cuisine" is born. ("Molecular gastronomy" is a term widely applied to this style of cooking, but no one who cooks it actually likes the term; "modernist cuisine" becomes an acceptable middle ground in the late 2000s.) The team will eventually grow to fifty members, but initially includes Ferran and Albert Adrià, Bixente Arrieta, Àlvaro Martínez, and Andoni Luis Adúriz. Oriol Castro, René Redzepi, José Andrés, and Grant Achatz will all put in time at El Bulli.

After leaving his New York restaurant Rakel in 1990 (where he was named Best New Chef by *Food & Wine*) and spending several years at Checkers Hotel in Los Angeles, Thomas Keller buys the French Laundry (on a tip from Jonathan Waxman).

1995

Marco Pierre White wins his third Michelin star, making him the youngest chef (and first Englishman) to do so. Heston Blumenthal opens the Fat Duck in Bray, England. Blumenthal pursues a path of modernist cooking that will influence chefs around the globe and help establish him as one of the most influential British chefs of the next two decades.

1996

Joël Robuchon, Georges Blanc, Bernard Loiseau, and Alain Ducasse sign a manifesto to "save French cuisine," which they feel has been threatened by globalization. Marc Veyrat organizes a group of French chefs including Michel Bras, Alain Passard, and Michel Troisgros, and they write their own manifesto, to "be open to the world." Nationalism is at the heart of both manifestos: Veyrat says cuisine "must again become the ambassador of our heritage." In the next five years, the *New Yorker* and *Time* both run stories on "the crisis of haute cuisine" as the French fear losing their supremacy in fine dining.

1997

Reichl calls Jean Georges "an entirely new kind of four-star restaurant," crediting Jean-Georges Vongerichten with "a restaurant revolution." He brings global eclecticism to the table within a haute-French model and is widely imitated.

1998

Alain Ducasse becomes the first chef in over fifty years to hold six Michelin stars at the same time—three for Alain Ducasse au Plaza Athénée in Paris, and three for Le Louis XV in Monte Carlo.

1999

Marc Veyrat, building on the success of his first restaurant, L'Auberge de l'Eridan, spends twenty million francs building and opening La Ferme de mon Père in the Haute-Savoie region of France, a massive restaurant in the style of a Savoyard farmhouse, where he uses modernist techniques to showcase the region's flora.

2001

Alain Passard takes the bold step of removing red meat and seafood from the menu at his restaurant L'Arpège in Paris, effectively pushing the principles of nouvelle cuisine to their logical extreme and helping to redirect the culinary world's attention to vegetables. A year later he buys a farm, setting the new standard for restaurants concerned with the quality of their produce.

2002

Restaurant magazine starts the World's 50 Best Restaurants list, which will later become a stand-alone enterprise partnered with San Pellegrino. Though the list has detractors (Fred Morin and David McMillan of Joe Beef refer to restaurants in its purview as "bottled water restaurants"), it inarguably brings many chefs and restaurants from outside the Michelin fold into the international conversation about cuisine.

2003

L'Atelier de Joël Robuchon begins serving guests at intimate "chef's counters" inspired by Japanese service, a rethinking of what constitutes fine dining service. Chefs around the world will imitate this in the years that follow.

After training at El Bulli and the French Laundry, René Redzepi returns home to Copenhagen to open Noma, the restaurant he hoped would define Nordic cooking through the use of its produce. Seven years later it will be named the best restaurant in the world by the World's 50 Best Restaurants, replacing El Bulli. (Michelin consistently awards it two stars.)

Chef Bernard Loiseau kills himself, allegedly because of rumors that his restaurant, La Côte d'Or, would lose its third Michelin star. The tragedy brings to light the intense pressure chefs face to achieve and retain their ratings.

2005

Michelin releases its first North American guide, for New York City. Four restaurants receive three stars: Alain Ducasse at the Essex House, Jean Georges, Le Bernardin, and Per Se. It is the beginning of run of global expansion that undercuts the almost holy authority of Michelin as an arbiter of taste. For instance, in the same year, Alain Senderens, chef of the three-star Lucas Carton in Paris, decides to take the restaurant in a more informal direction and return his stars to Michelin, labeling them "old-fashioned, outdated." Michelin's director, Jean-Luc Naret, tells the *Times*: "There is an interesting tendency with the chefs who think the stars belong to them. They belong to Michelin first."

2006

Iñaki Aizpitarte opens Le Chateaubriand, leading a movement toward more relaxed dining in Paris. Around the world, more chefs coming out of top-tier kitchens open less formal restaurants than those they trained in, but continue to cook in a way that pushes boundaries.

2008

Chef Santi Santamaría decries the modernist cooking of Adrià and his squad, setting off a debate within Spain—and later around the world—about cooking in old versus new styles, "natural" versus not. This will ultimately bring about the end of the modernist cooking style as the vanguard of cuisine, although its techniques and ingredients are now firmly part of the fine dining kitchen.

2010

Del Posto, owned by Mario Batali and Joseph and Lidia Bastianich, with chef Mark Ladner in the kitchen, becomes the first Italian restaurant to receive four stars from the *New York Times* since Parioli Romanissimo in 1974.

2011

Nathan Myhrvold, former chief technology officer for Microsoft, spends hundreds of thousands of dollars to self-publish the six-volume *Modernist Cuisine*.

In July, El Bulli has its last service.

Restaurateur Danny Meyer sells Eleven Madison Park to chef Daniel Humm and general manager Will Guidara just as EMP receives its third Michelin star. Meyer, whose restaurants have helped shape the path of fine dining in New York City since 1985, will become a force in fast food; Guidara and Humm will rocket up the World's 50 Best Restaurants list.

In the *New York Times*, Julia Moskin writes that Noma's influence has saturated the United States: "Evidence of the Nordic invasion is everywhere, once diners know the signs: cellared vegetables, unripe fruit, conifers, buttermilk and whey; rocks, shells and twigs used as serving pieces; garden scraps like radish leaves, turnip tails and nasturtium pods whorled, piled and clustered on the plate as if by waves or wind."

2013

Time publishes "The Gods of Food," featuring Alex Atala, David Chang, and René Redzepi. The issue—and the cover—gains notoriety for its lack of female chefs. Perhaps just as interesting, however, is that the cover includes a chef from South America, a chef of Muslim heritage, and one of Korean descent. Nobody's French or cooking food that is recognizably French. **LP**

The Sweet Science

BY DAVID CHANG

To me, there is no better analogy for fine dining than boxing.

The comparison starts outside of the ring, with training and dedication and preparation and the choice to pursue the path. There is no room for a halfhearted boxer. When you sign up, you are signing up for a beating, for countless years in gyms and weight rooms and at the other end of another guy's gloved fists.

For the past hundred years or so, the only path to the top of the best kitchens has been paved with the promise of giving away every waking hour of the better part of your early adulthood. Most of the hours will be spent being bad at the task you are doing, and there will be a generation of men standing over you who will let you know you are a fuckup in creatively abusive terms. From hauling incredibly heavy and hot things to doing tiny, precise cold work, you will be expected to be excellent and obedient and fast. Your ego will be black and blue by day two.

Even if you can manage the commitment, there's more than will or strength required to get into the ring. If that's all it took, every oversized knuckle-dragging genetic misfit could be a boxer. The sport requires speed, strategy, precision, focus, technique, a particular kind of smarts—and to get to a point where they put a shiny belt on you, you need those things in quantities that other people don't have. If you weren't born with them—and few are—that's a whole lot of extra work for your brain to do when your body's already pushed to the max.

It's not that different in the kitchen: everybody's compensating for what they don't have. You have to adapt to each new fight, learn a lexicon of techniques particular to the cuisines and kitchens that you work in. My hands are garbage compared

ILLUSTRATION BY ROB ENGVALL

to many cooks'. If all you have are knife skills or a killer left hook, somebody's going to come along with a more complete package and lay you out cold. I had to think about food and restaurants and how to get ahead, because no one was ever going to promote me on the merits of my kitchen skills alone.

And let's say you've got those things, the will and some modicum of talent that keeps you upright through the training process. Guess what? There are untold piles of bullshit that accompany you on the way to practice what you do: all the promoters and profiteers, the Don Kings and Bob Arums of the game. As a chef, no one prepares you for publicists and investors and a whole class of criminals who know how to profit off of people, and know that if you're not willing to play, another kid will pop up with the same dreams next week or next month.

Once you've run that gauntlet, what you get is a chance to get your ass kicked every time you go out. But that's when all your training kicks in. You do it. You feint and jab and see lighting-fast punches in slow motion and duck out of the way. You take the carcass of a dead animal and turn it into poetry. If you've done everything right in the lifetime leading up to those moments, you swing and connect and you win. It's worth it, because you've decided it's worth it, and if there are legions of people who think your choice is invalid—that boxing is brutality, that refined cooking is pointless frippery—then that's on them, not on you.

But the real connection between boxing and cooking occurred to me when Muhammad Ali died. Most people under forty didn't seem to care, or they didn't care in the way the generation who saw him as the heavyweight champion of the world did—who saw him as a conscientious objector to the Vietnam War, as a poet

and a leader and an icon. Ali's death mattered to my dad and grandpa—he was an idol to them—so it mattered to me. While this is, of course, a function of age, it's also a function of what's happened to boxing: it is no longer central, it is no longer a part of our national dialogue.

Fifty years ago, that would have been *unthinkable*. If what happened to Deontay Wilder happened during the early years of the Cold War, we might've fired missiles. I'm imagining you have no idea who Deontay Wilder is. When the most legitimate American heavyweight prospect in at least a decade missed out on the biggest fight of his career because his Russian nemesis got caught doping, hardly anyone noticed or cared. Today, kids idolize UFC guys with face tattoos in cage matches. If they're going to practice something that involves hitting another human, it's far more likely to be Brazilian jiujitsu or an Asian martial art. This is the march of time. Boxing still exists, sure, and I'm sure there are some great guys out there lacing up the gloves. But the days when their names rang out like Rocky Marciano or Joe Louis or Joe Frazier? Gone.

And that's what's happened with fine dining. There was a time—and I know because I came up in it—when fine dining was the only game in town worth playing. To be at the helm of a three-Michelin-star restaurant was to be a heavyweight champ; fine dining was the highest level of achievement in my field. I'd talk about which chefs stole which chefs' dishes with the same excitement kids used to recount Ali and Frazier at the Thrilla in Manila.

At the present moment, the generation that's entering kitchens and culinary school is growing up in a world where there's greater access to better food than ever before. (And of course we're talking about people in food-secure situations here; fine

dining is the purview of the rich and pretend-rich.) There are a dozen different ways to gain notoriety and put dinner on the table. You can study Muay Thai, Brazilian jiujitsu, judo, Greco-Roman wrestling, karate. Even within boxing, the welterweight and middleweight divisions have become more profitable and interesting than the heavyweights.

For a long time, if you were a fighter and you wanted to make it on the world stage, you had to be a heavyweight boxer. That was where the talent went. For a long time in the Western world, you had a consolidation of talent in fine dining. The concentration of talent made it so that fine dining restaurants served the food that you *had* to want. Sure, there were other styles of food. But if you were really good, you weren't going to open up a barbecue place or do take-out, you were going to work for the best.

All of this is not to say that people in fine dining aren't doing good work. They are! And they're still going to do great work. I just believe the great work being done in fine dining today is an anomaly. It is the work of people who have chosen the punishing path of the sweet science and the limited rewards it offers them. Fine dining was once the only place to go, the only way to do things, and today it is just another mode of cooking.

Things have changed. There are options. *Wait a second, I don't want to serve fine dining, this is stupid, I just want to make food. If I just want to make food, why do I have to do it in a fine dining environment, why do I have to cater to these people?* People should embrace that. People should embrace the pluralism and the diversity. It's exciting that there are many avenues to eat well. But there will not be another Bocuse, another Muhammad Ali, not in the way that those giants once strode across society. That time has passed. **LP**

Listen at 101 Greene Street.
New York, NY

SONOS
The Home Sound System

sonos.com/nyc

The Nobility of Service
A defense of fine dining

by Will Guidara

I believe in the nobility of fine dining. But eleven years ago, I wanted nothing to do with it.

I grew up in restaurants. My dad was a restaurateur, and I always wanted to be in the business, but I never wanted to be in the kitchen—I wanted to be in the dining room.

I discovered when I was very young that taking responsibility for others' experiences was something that I cared about, that I felt fulfilled by. A lot of chefs will say, "I wasn't a super social person, and I liked being in the kitchen." But for me, from an early age, I just loved entertaining people. I'm the type of person who loves Christmas more for the gifts I give than the ones I receive. It's equally selfish, in a way— you just like watching what your gift does to someone.

I can trace the start of it back to when I was six, when my mom got brain cancer. By the time I was twelve, she was a quadriplegic. My dad moved us to a house a few blocks

from my school, because I no longer had someone to drive me around, where my mom's bedroom could be on the ground floor. But the house had a second floor, and it was mine. This was entirely by my dad's design: he wanted me to have that safe place, that ability to have a hub for my social life and one that kept me safe and close to the family. That space, my space, was the best for entertaining. All my friends were always over at my house.

It was at that point in my life that I decided what I wanted to do: study hospitality at the Cornell University School of Hotel Administration and go into the restaurant business. (This to the chagrin of my family, who

ILLUSTRATIONS BY JOSE MIGUEL MENDEZ

wanted me to be a banker or a lawyer or something else upstanding and professional.) Once I was in college, I spent summers working for the best restaurants I could, because I wanted to learn from the best, including Drew Nieporent at Tribeca Grill and Wolfgang Puck and Barbara Lazaroff at the recently relocated Spago, in Beverly Hills. At those places I saw over-the-top gestures unlike anything I'd previously imagined.

At the original West Hollywood Spago, there was a regular named Marvin Davis, the owner of 20th Century Fox—he'd have lunch there pretty much five days a week. Barbara went to Marvin's house when he wasn't there, asked his wife what his favorite chair was, took a ton of pictures of it, and had a furniture maker make that chair and upholster it in Spago fabric. My shifts always started with making sure Marvin's chair was at his table. That is insane! And it's amazing. Did Marvin love that chair? Sure. Did Wolfgang and Barbara love the idea that they'd given him the chair? Probably even more.

I love opportunities to do things outside of what anyone could possibly expect, to create the sort of experience that turns into a story that gets told over and over again. I had one of my first nights like that after the end of my senior year at Cornell.

At school there was an amazing guest-chefs class, where chefs would come and the students would cook and wait tables and market and sell the event. You got to meet good people. I was in charge of marketing, which meant I was also in charge of entertaining the chefs when they came up. Daniel Boulud sent up his team—Neil Gallagher, Johnny Iuzzini, and a couple others—the day before he got there, and I took care of them—nothing fancy, just beer and food and the sort of night out that college kids like to have.

When Daniel arrived the next day, I had been preordained by his guys. And that night, we had a huge party after the dinner at my college house. Daniel and I raided the hotel kitchen; he commandeered pans and eggs and truffles and caviar and brought them back to my house at 130 College Avenue, where we had a couple kegs of Milwaukee's Best. He started cooking for everyone and serving caviar. It was the greatest night of all those college kids' lives, especially at Cornell, where everyone's super into it. At the end of the night he told me, *Hey, you should come to the restaurant.*

This was 2001. My mom passed away the day after graduation, and I was leaving for Spain a month later. The night before I left, I took Daniel up on his invitation, and my dad and I drove down from Boston to New York. We changed in a gas station on the way there.

You walk in the doors of a place like Daniel and it's intimidating, exciting. They brought us right through the dining room, into the kitchen, and up to the Skybox—a walled-in glass booth that overlooks the kitchen. Daniel talked to us the entire night through the intercom from the pass. The GM served us all the courses—it was something like fifteen. Daniel stayed until the very end, comped the meal, and gave us a tour of the entire restaurant.

Here was this place that was so crazy, high-end, fine dining, expensive. I was a college kid. I had given him a keg of beer—there was nothing more he could ever expect to get from me. But he decided that he wanted to make it an amazing night for me. And it was the first time in my life that I was able to give my dad an experience that *he* had never had before. That meal will forever be one of the most important nights of my life. And walking out of that restaurant that night, all I wanted to do was

to be able to create experiences like that for other people.

But as I got more experience working in restaurants, I saw that at a certain level—at many fine dining restaurants—you end up with a chef who thinks the only thing that matters is what he or she does. As the dining-room guy you have to convince them that what you care about matters as much as what they care about. That didn't work for me: I couldn't control both sides of the equation, and I didn't see a path forward that wouldn't be a constant battle.

I worked for Danny Meyer at Tabla for a while, then left and worked at Restaurant Associates, a big food-service company. It was like getting my graduate degree: for two years I worked five a.m. to five p.m. I did all the purchasing in the morning and the controlling work in the afternoon.

One afternoon while visiting an old coworker at Union Square Cafe, I ran into Danny Meyer, and we struck up a conversation, which ultimately led to an e-mail exchange where he said, *Hey, we just signed a deal to do the restaurants at MoMA, we should talk.*

I told him I wanted to work with him again, but I didn't want anything to do with fine dining. So I signed on to be the GM of the cafés at MoMA, and it was the best. I got to design parts of the Museum of Modern Art! Around that time, Danny decided Eleven Madison Park needed to be better, and he hired Daniel Humm from Campton Place.

The person running the front of house wasn't the right fit with Daniel, and he asked Danny, *What about Will?* Because we'd seen each other at weekly meetings. I was like, *Dude, I don't want anything to do with fine dining!* But we decided that I'd go for a year, because my dad said, *Hey, if you want to grow with the company and they want something from you, you should give it to them, and then they'll be there for you when you need them.*

But when Daniel and I started working together, everything changed. I realized that if he could bring his three-Michelin-star experience (from Le Pont de Brent, in Switzerland) and I could bring all my experience, which was very different, and together we could do something different—it didn't have to be stuffy, it could be fun.

Some people come into our restaurant, Eleven Madison Park, because they are really into food and they want to experience Daniel's newest creations, see what he's up to, see if he's as good as some review said he was. For others, fine dining is the exclamation point at the end of an accomplishment, the scene for their celebration. I recently got a letter from a man who had his fiftieth birthday with us. He knew he wanted to celebrate at a restaurant; he spent months trying to figure out where he wanted to go, and he saved up for it. Eventually he chose Eleven Madison Park and trusted us with this important night. A few weeks later, he wrote a two-page letter about how the meal was more than dinner, it was about giving himself the grace to be truly cared for.

There are some people who come to forget things. Life is hard, and sometimes you need to go into a bubble where everything's perfect for a little while. Fine dining should be make-believe; it should be the world as you wish it existed.

Also, I came to fine dining to take care of people. There's nowhere else where you have the time and resources to really take care of people. I think hospitality can exist in all forms of restaurants if people decide that it's important to them. I think it can exist at a McDonald's, at a Shake Shack, a diner, a noodle bar. But the highest fulfillment of what it can be is not possible in a five-minute transaction.

The chef from the Clove Club, in London, came to EMP with his guys. He was a fishmonger when he was a kid and loved crab racing. We set up a course in the kitchen, bought a bunch of crabs, hand-painted numbers, had everyone pick a number, and did a fucking crab race in the kitchen. As soon as it was over, we pulled the tablecloth that we'd painted with the finish line and the starting line to reveal a layer of newspaper, and then we dumped a crab boil on the table.

When a family from Spain was dining with us, it started snowing—it was the first time their kids had seen snow. When they left, we had an Uber SUV waiting with sleds to take them to Central Park. A diner was joking with his server about his love of Cheez-Its, so we served them an extra course of caviar and Cheez-Its. You need the world of fine dining in order to be able to do those things (and I need a chef who is willing to do things like serve a box of Cheez-Its!).

None of this would be possible at restaurants that a) don't have the time, and b) don't have the resources, the staff, the money, the supplies, and the ability. Beyond the

dining room, we have the time and space and resources to have R&D chefs, and all these people who can really work to develop all these new techniques that make a guest's experience better, and simultaneously evolve the craft of cooking.

At MoMA and at Tabla, I took care of people in a very different way—it was the same motivation but expressed differently. I'm a thoroughbred when I have a fine dining stage to work on. In casual restaurants I was able to brighten people's day, and I was able to exceed their expectations, but in fine dining I'm able to create one of the best nights of someone's entire life. And that's a very different thing.

That's my responsibility. It's what I believe gives nobility to the craft of service. Sure, Eleven Madison Park is expensive, and that seems to be the only thing about fine dining that people focus on anymore, but since when is something being expensive such an ugly thing?

People talk about restaurants as playgrounds for the rich, but *Hamilton* is expensive, too, and no one thinks that only rich people are going to see *Hamilton*. People shouldn't hate the idea of fine dining just because it's expensive or because they think it's exclusionary. That's judging something without allowing yourself the opportunity to get to know it.

If you save up your money for something special, you can buy a nicer stereo system, get a nicer car, go to the theater and sit next to the person that you love and not talk to each other. Or, you can take a few hours of your life and create a memory. That's the business I am in: of creating those moments, of making the impossible possible, at least for a few hours.

When I went to Mugaritz for the first time, there were two cards on the table: one was 150 MINUTES... SUBMIT!, the other was 150 MINUTES... REBEL! I was given the choice to either enjoy or protest. It seemed like you were going to have different meals depending on which card you picked. In reality, it had no impact. It was a statement: *Hey, right now, before you even start, where are you at? Are you here to enjoy yourself, or are you here to hate? Because if you're here to hate, nothing we can do is gonna make this good for you.*

The moment when diners and critics walk into a restaurant with the intention of disliking it, it's dangerous for fine dining. The experience requires a commitment from the person delivering it *and* from the person receiving it. No matter how awesome what I do is, unless you're choosing to enjoy it, it's never going to work.

It's half about what we're serving and half the grace that people are giving themselves to receive it. I think that growing cynicism could kill fine dining altogether without even recognizing what it's doing. And I don't think we want a world without fine dining. There wouldn't be these places for people to go to forget about the world outside, these places that can be magical in a world that increasingly needs a little magic. **LP**

Cook
Ch

s & efs

The State of Fine Dining

We talked to some of the world's best chefs about fine dining's potential and its problems, its past, present, and future.

Illustrations by
Jaci Kessler Lubliner

We struggled from the beginning to define fine dining. Even the French, who essentially invented the thing, don't really have a term for it. It's much easier to make declarations about its condition—Fine dining is dead! Fine dining has changed! Fine dining is taking a nap!—than it is to say exactly what fine dining is.

So here are eighteen far-flung chefs answering simple but tough questions about their industry—where the ship is headed, where it's been, who's on board, why anyone should care. They represent a squad that is Taylor Swiftian in its caliber (but hopefully a shade more diverse in its composition): a little bit of the old guard, some young guns, the keepers of the flame, world movers, Californians, Chicagoans, New Yorkers, the French, expats, a New Zealander, and a Dane. We enlisted our elite team of global super friends to track down a few of the more elusive specimens in this collection. Christine Muhlke interviewed Yannick Alléno; Kevin Pang spoke to Grant Achatz and Noah Sandoval; Karen Leibowitz chatted with Dominique Crenn; and Alex Toledano managed to pin down Iñaki Aizpitarte and Olivier Roellinger in Paris. We've merged everyone's answers into one big chorus, but their opinions aren't always harmonious. At the end of the day, that's the beauty of fine dining: people from opposite corners of the planet working with the same fanatical dedication, motivated by wildly different reasons.

What is fine dining, exactly?

Christopher Kostow, The Restaurant at Meadowood (St. Helena, California): Service is paramount in fine dining. An understanding of food and wine and their relationship is paramount. I think a space that has some inherent beauty is paramount. It doesn't necessarily need to have chandeliers or whatever, but I think it really needs to represent, in all its facets, the beautiful things of life—the same way that going to a symphony or going to a play is a meeting of high culture and consumer. Fine dining is opera; it's well-executed jazz.

Dominique Crenn, Atelier Crenn (San Francisco): It might be a little bit more expensive, but you have this sense of hospitality, this sense that it's catered just for the guests that come. Maybe you get more service; perhaps you can eat food that you don't eat every day. You feel *pampered*. That would be the word.

Daniel Humm, Eleven Madison Park (New York): As amazing as the past few years have been for chefs and restaurants, the one thing that's been overlooked is the craft of service. It hasn't been celebrated, and I think there are people out there who work on perfecting hospitality and service—all the stuff that's such an art and requires such an effort. Seeing somebody decant the beautiful bottle of wine and doing a tableside tea service or cutting a chicken in front of you—how beautiful is that? At Eleven Madison Park we definitely believe in it.

Noah Sandoval, Oriole (Chicago): The epitome of fine dining is comforting people and wowing people and making them feel special, as opposed to: *We have food, we serve you food, see you next time.*

David Kinch, Manresa (Los Gatos, California): I just went to Louis XV in Monaco a couple months ago, day of the Grand Prix—I watched the Grand Prix from the terrace and ate after. It could very well be the oldest and stuffiest restaurant around, but instead it's *dynamic*. The dining room is one of the greatest rooms of the nineteenth century, with the walls and the murals and all the gilt—all that is fussy and boring and dead. With the objects they've placed in the room, and the workstations, and what they wear, and the food that is served, they honor all of that, yet it's so twenty-first century, and so of the *now*. To me, that's fine dining. Fine dining evolves just like everything else.

Iñaki Aizpitarte, Le Chateaubriand (Paris): In France, we know that we'll have an experience both of cooking and of service with a very substantial investment—very inspired and very controlled. We know that every detail, down to the millimeter, will be attended to and that the customer will be led around by the nose from beginning to end. Not much is left for improvisation. On the other hand, many other approaches to fine dining are getting invented in models other than the French. Here we are under the impression of having a model that is a bit more professional. A bit more reduced. I don't want to say that it's the same all the time, because when you are at someone's place you are specifically at his or her place, but there is still a thread.

Olivier Roellinger, Les Maisons de Bricourt (Cancale, France): Fine dining is for me, above all, the coherence between a moment and a place. This makes me think of a potato.

It's eight in the morning right now. We are going to dig up new potatoes. The dirt is warmer than the air. We feel the dirt, we stick our hands in and mix it up and pull out this little bonbon from the earth. There is already a smell—it's completely magical. After cooking them in a bit of water, lightly salted, we'll enjoy them with a thick knob of salted butter—churned, raw-milk butter—crushed with our fork. It should be eaten on a wood table by the sea. At the moment, this, for me, is the best lunch.

> Seeing somebody decant the beautiful bottle of wine and doing a tableside tea service or cutting a chicken in front of you—how beautiful is that? —Daniel Humm

The climax of the *dégustation* of flavors is the moment that crystallizes the *bonheur* of a moment in a specific place, because even the most delicious, refined dish—I have a fondness for those by Michel Bras, or by Pierre Gagnaire, or by the Troisgros, or by René Redzepi—comes from the cuisine of its place.

Grant Achatz, Alinea (Chicago): Let's say you're sitting at the sushi counter at Jiro, and all you do is eat sushi, and then you're gone in forty-five minutes because he kicks you out. Is that fine dining? I think it is. If you go to Thailand and eat Indian food at Gaggan, that's certainly fine dining. There's a certain amount of respect for quality of ingredients. There has to be good cooking, delicious food. That being said, you can find that at a place like Fat Rice [a Macanese restaurant in Chicago], as well. It's a really difficult question to answer.

André Soltner, Dean of Classic Studies, International Culinary Center (New York): Today we have too many people who go to expensive restaurants because it's chic, and that's what they call fine dining. For me, fine dining is when you sit down and you enjoy your food very, very much. For me, fine dining is to use the best ingredients, not sophisticated, the simplest possible, and all the rest comes after.

Joshua Skenes, Saison (San Francisco): I think that we should have restaurants that are either good or not good. That should be our focus, because the lines are much more blurred now. People are trying to do fancy food in more casual environments. A restaurant should focus on being the best of its kind, at every price point. All the rest is irrelevant. The only thing that really matters to me is that you come in, you have a good time, you receive hospitality, and you don't get the silliness. The silliness is when you go into a restaurant that is very busy and they treat you like a commodity. The silliness is that kind of *No, go away, we're busy* attitude.

Ben Shewry, Attica (Melbourne): I guess when I think of the words *fine dining,* I think of the French three-Michelin-star classic restaurant more than I think of my own restaurant. It's not really a tag that I love, to be honest. That's the tag that society's cast upon ambitious restaurants like Attica or Noma or Osteria Francescana.

René Redzepi, Noma (Copenhagen): All the gastronomical terms we have—*local* or *molecular gastronomy* or *farm-to-table*—once you dig in to them, they don't mean anything. For instance, at Noma we're considered "local," but our urchin is from two thousand kilometers away. The terms are bullshit. Fine dining, casual dining, fast food. I think what Rosio Sanchez is doing [at Hija de Sanchez] in Copenhagen is fine dining to me. They wake up every day and cook everything with the best ingredients they can get. They cook it fresh and they serve it with generosity.

I mean, what is fine dining supposed to be? A very slow dinner? Maybe in the past, fine dining meant a specific type of restaurant, where you'd get the best food. But that's not true any more. Today, the best food sometimes is actually at Rosio's or Superiority Burger, where you can have freshly cooked broccoli from the same market where the Per Se chefs shop.

One thing I do hate about this whole discussion is that it's always either/or, which I think is so stupid. There's room for restaurants of all genres, and it's a great thing that people can have delicious meals more affordably. I also think many more people in the future will save up a little extra to go and have a fine dining experience. Tasting-menu restaurants aren't over—I don't think that at all. I think all the foodies

The epitome of fine dining is comforting people and wowing people and making them feel special, as opposed to: We have food, we serve you food, see you next time.
—Noah Sandoval

The best fine dining is delicious, usually something you haven't seen before, and thought-provoking. It's more than just sustenance. You're eating ideas.
—David Kinch

growing up right now—there are millions and millions—will want to have them around.

Does fine dining still matter as much now as it used to?

Kinch: Of course it does. Where do ideas come from? The top, and they trickle down. It's like the design of a taillight on a Ferrari. It looks like it's a spaceship, it doesn't make sense, and it's beautiful. Six years later, every Acura and every Honda Civic in the world has that feature. The ideas happen in restaurants where they feed forty people a night, where there's a lot of labor involved. Just because you can't afford fine dining, or you reject the notion, doesn't make it obsolete.

Kostow: Fine dining restaurants are the laboratories in which so much innovation is happening, and in some cases it can only happen in those kitchens because of the size of the staff and the financial investment that's being made in those operations. I think it's more relevant now than it ever has been—I really do.

Redzepi: I would not be spending sixteen hours a day cooking for forty people if I didn't feel there was a greater purpose than just making these forty people happy. I don't necessarily consider Noma a traditional restaurant. I see it more as a place where we experiment with things—techniques, ingredients, ideas—and the guests get to try it. Would I want to go to work, would I ask my team to

work sixteen-hour days for minimum pay if the sole purpose was to make money? I would say there are more clever ways to make money. Noma is a part of bringing forward a new restaurant culture for our region.

Shewry: It matters. I see why it matters every day with my young guys, but also almost every night with cooks who come in to eat. But I do think things are a little bit different than they used to be. I think a lot of young cooks look at Attica and see it as some crazy unattainable dream. And they think it's just too hard to start a restaurant like that without a lot of money, without backers. I mean the staffing levels at Attica—compared to a lot of other restaurants—is double. A lot of people seem to be going an easier route, something that's more achievable, something that's more casual.

Achatz: It's more relevant now, because it lacks so much definition. I don't think anyone can say fine dining isn't relevant, because defining fine dining is becoming more difficult.

Crenn: The diner needs to have some type of choice. That's what the culinary world is about: you can have a taco on the side of the street, or you go to a nice place and you can eat an incredible meal, or you can go to a burger bar. It's about diversity. It's like if you go to a movie and can only see

action movies. You need cerebral movies, you need movies that make you think; you need cartoons, or you need comedies, or you need dramas. You need diversity to balance the industry.

Roellinger: Of course I hope a restaurant like Taillevent will always exist, because it's just like how the great masters of sushi in Japan exist today. It's important that there remain temples that embody and mark an era. It is wonderful to say that we can go eat an amazing vol-au-vent. It's something that I don't have any idea how to make, but that I am very happy to go eat.

Aizpitarte: We don't need to see these places disappear, nor imagine that they might disappear. I became a chef late, and my idea was to create a cooking style that I did not yet fully grasp but that would let me move forward and listen to my desires and everything. I was attracted by these Parisian spaces where you were able to immerse a customer in a place—where they were used to going, where they were immediately

Luxury, for me, is about someone taking care of you beautifully. It's not about giving you a five-hundred-dollar glass of champagne. It's about a human connection. —Dominique Crenn

relaxed, almost at home. They create a different welcome and give the bistro feeling to a customer, even if I am not trying to run a bistro. We popularized the term *bistronomie*. I think that it is going to balance out between bistronomie and high-level fine dining restaurants. It used to be very categorical—there was fine dining, bistros, and bistronomie. I think that the barriers will break down and everyone will find their spot.

Achatz: What we're seeing is what we always see: the ebb and flow of opinion. There was a strong kickback to fine dining five, seven years ago, which I directly attribute to chefs like David Chang and Michael Carlson—guys that had grown up in fine dining restaurants such as Daniel, Alain Ducasse, and the French Laundry. They were chefs in the grind of those environments and hours and seriousness, and they got tired of it. They said, "When I open my own place, I just want to cook, I don't care if it's on fine china or using foie gras." Then

came the popularity of places like Momofuku and Schwa. And everyone said fine dining was dead! And then you see the younger cooks from Momofuku and Schwa have themselves gone into fine dining. They're not doing classic French food, they're doing something a bit more pricey and a bit more refined, because cooks want to do the opposite of their mentors.

How has the industry changed during your career? How would you like to see it continue to evolve?

Soltner: In my generation, th chef was in the kitchen. Today, it's changed a little bit, but I don't criticize that, because if I were still in the restaurant business, maybe I would do the same thing. But fifty years ago, the chef was there. My generation, you had one restaurant you were in charge of. But today, you have restaurants where you can have a very, very good meal, and the chef-owner is not behind the stove. Maybe thirty, forty, fifty years ago, if you had a restaurant, you made an okay living. Maybe today you need two or three to make a good living.

Shewry: When I came to Melbourne in 2002, it was just after a period of great, small, chef-run, chef-owned fine

dining restaurants had closed. There was one place called Est Est Est, which was a very famous Melbourne restaurant—very, very high-end in terms of what it was doing. There was another one called Pom, which was of a similar kind of ambition and level. Andrew McConnell still had a really ambitious small restaurant then, but he closed that, as well.

Back then, it still felt like you could build a restaurant over time into what you wanted it to be, but now there are more reviewers, more publications, countless websites. You've got all these systems of determining what is a good restaurant and what is a crap restaurant, and I don't think people feel like they have the freedom or the time to take the risk to develop into a fine dining restaurant.

That's not going to change, though. Our desire right now is for newness all the time. I just want to see more cooks and more waiters empowered to open their own places by themselves. That's what I really want to see. I don't like to bring it back to the World's 50 Best, but if you look at that list of restaurants, you see the vast majority of them are independently owned restaurants. The chef or the front-of-house team own it and they work in it and it's individual, and that's what I like.

Kostow: As an industry, we're always looking at what's new, and we've lost a lot of the history. No one uses butters and cream and all that stuff anymore, which is fine. No one does silver-cloche service, which is fine. But have we ever asked ourselves why not? Why did we go from plating the food in a tight little circle to plating the food with wood sorrel all over the place? We plated the food in a tight circle because that's what Thomas did in *The French Laundry Cookbook.* We went all wood-sorrel-y because that's what René did. We're building on things that happened in the last twenty years. I think chefs are going to start looking further back and asking ourselves why we have rid ourselves of certain things. I think that enables us to teach our staff a lot better and enables us to maintain the history of our industry a lot better.

Achatz: When I graduated from culinary school, the epitome of fine dining was Alain Ducasse and Joël Robuchon and the French chefs. I remember going to France, telling myself, *I'm going to the holy land,* and I remember being incredibly disappointed. It was technically perfect and gluttonous in every way, but it wasn't expressive or personal. By the time I got to the French Laundry, food in the nineties was both expressive and incredibly intellectual, and it was fusion—using, say, Moroccan or Japanese spices—which was something new. That was the start of emotional cooking. Then you get to the 1980s and '90s, and here come the Spaniards. You got Ferran, Andoni, Arzak doing this food that people didn't know what to think of—you either loved it or hated it, but it was certainly new. Then, we're intentionally trying to avoid luxury ingredients, saying the potato is just as important as the lobster tail, like Noma, and this is happening at the same time as a place like Schwa, playing death metal in the dining room and taking shots of Jameson.

Where we're at now, you have a blend of everything. What you're seeing is diversity in fine dining. You go to France and can still go to Alain Ducasse, you can come to Alinea and get emotional, theatrical fine dining, you can go to Noma and get that version of fine dining. Where's it going? I think there'll be a resurgence of classicism. I think you'll see some of those old French-style restaurants come back—tableside boning of Dover sole, elaborate soufflés, ornate desserts. But I also think the blending and diversification will continue.

Sandoval: When I was a teenager, things were a bit more stuffy, a bit more scripted, at least in my world. I grew up in Richmond, Virginia, and D.C. was the best place I could eat. Even when I moved to Chicago eight years ago, things were still different from today. Servers were instructed to act a specific way, chefs were assholes, sous chefs were even bigger assholes, and cooks were overworked. Nobody seemed to care about camaraderie. Now, I think that's dying. Especially in Chicago, people are being treated with more respect. We're essentially equals here. A lot more younger people are running restaurants, and that's a good and bad thing.

Aizpitarte: There are institutions that will not change, like the Maison Troisgros, which gets passed from father to son. That is one category among many others in fine dining. But I think that fundamentally, for young people who are attracted to this type of thing, this type of fine dining, this idea, it is bound to evolve. We are seeing fewer people taking care of tables, fewer servers. But these historic restaurants must evolve, like bistros evolved, like ways of eating have evolved.

I think that we are right at the heart of an evolution. For generations,

I think there'll be a resurgence of classicism. I think you'll see some of those old French-style restaurants come back—tableside boning of Dover sole, elaborate soufflés, ornate desserts. But I also think the blending and diversification will continue.
—Grant Achatz

Relaxed doesn't mean not professional! —Iñaki Aizpitarte

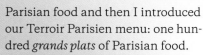

people have been used to these codes, these expectations. It is clear that there are gaps and that they haven't been capitalized on, but there will be an equilibrium soon. As people have moved on to something else, fine dining has been reinvented. It's been done maybe more abroad, as in France we really have a more traditional culture of fine dining. But many people who like to try the great restaurants also want to go to a more relaxed fine dining restaurant. Relaxed doesn't mean not professional!

Kinch: I hear from a lot of guests that nobody wants to commit four hours to a dinner. I don't. My ass starts to hurt, and my attention starts to flag after three hours, I just start getting tired. I think you're going to see more à la carte options. Fine dining restaurants in France have tasting menus, but they've always had à la carte options. A lot of times that's the way to go over there: larger plates become more complex, ideas become more realized because it's not two bites, three bites. It's not like eating *mise en place*, which a lot of tasting menus are. All the dishes seem to be half-finished.

Alléno: In 2008, I was at Le Meurice. François Simon [former critic for *Le Figaro*] wrote an article about the chefs of my generation—Jean-François Piège, [Eric] Frechon, [Christian] Le Squer, and me—saying that he found my generation lacked personality. We all had the same reflexes, thanks to nouvelle cuisine. No individuality: we were all inspired by Ducasse's *Grand Livre de Cuisine*, we all did sous vide and plated in an aesthetically perfect way. The

nineties was the start of aestheticized food, so we were all inspired by it. He listed the names of dishes—all evocative of the phenomenon, with practically the same wording for each—and said, *Chefs, this weekend, your job is to find out where these dishes came from*. I took the paper, balled it up, threw it in the wastebasket. I hated it. In the evening, I came back after playing soccer with my kids in the Tuileries and reread it. I was angry, but I said, "Well, he's right. Obviously he's right." I said to myself, "Who are you, anyway?" I looked within.

I was born in the suburbs. Parisian kitchens were run by people from the provinces. In those communities, if you weren't Basque, Breton, or Auvergnat, you practically couldn't work. I could never say that I was a suburbanite, so for years I didn't tell people where I was from. Therefore, I was constrained in a thing that wasn't me. Simon's article made me understand who I was. My parents had a bistro. We moved every two years. So I did the tour of Paris. I didn't have childhood friends. I lived in so many neighborhoods. I wanted to say, *Okay, if I'm a Parisian, why can't I talk about Parisian food?* So I took out books. Parisian agriculture was once like Lyonnais agriculture: it was amazing! The guys were growing pumpkins at the feet of the Église Saint-Jacques just before the war. In Paris you ate cantal with butter, or oysters with butter, because it was the crossroads of provinces, so people enlisted in a kind of exchange. I looked for the history of

Parisian food and then I introduced our Terroir Parisien menu: one hundred *grands plats* of Parisian food.

Now we have just introduced le Principal [the main course] menu. For me, the main course is the thing around which the entire meal should unfold. We had an era where the main course—*main!*—was 30 percent of the duration of the meal. It was born with nouvelle cuisine. That's not normal. Why not put 70 percent of our attention on the main course and build on what the Spanish brought us in the 2000s: emotive cuisine?

Crenn: You have to bring people in, and you get to make them comfortable and also invite them into your world. Luxury, for me, is about someone taking care of you beautifully. It's not about giving you a five-hundred-dollar glass of champagne. It's about a human connection.

Kinch: There was a whole meme ten or fifteen years ago about, *Food doesn't need to be delicious, it just needs to be thought-provoking*. I completely reject that. Food has to taste good. It can still be thought-provoking. I can make food that tastes like shit that's interesting. That's easy to do. A lot of molecular gastronomy is that. The best fine dining is delicious, usually something you haven't seen before, *and* thought-provoking. It's more than just sustenance. You're eating ideas.

Redzepi: Today you can get a sorbet at Superiority Burger that's better than what most restaurants can make. I think fine dining will really have to start specializing, having a specific focus, instead of being a broad spectrum of everything.

I think that'll be an exciting future, where different restaurants are cooking different things at different parts of the year. Sometimes it can be a bit of the same, and that's a problem the guidebooks created. They increase the standard, but they also make everything very formulaic and very much the same. There used to be the obligatory slab of foie gras. There would be all the same ingredients invoked all the time; it was almost guaranteed to have pigeon or beef on the menu. Today, it's different, because everyone knows a decent butcher and can get a steak that's just as tender as the one they can get in a restaurant. I think we're all going to have to up our game. It's going to be harder, for sure. You'll have to really give people a reason to go to your restaurant. The fact that the meat is cooked perfectly won't be enough—everybody will be able to do that.

I think fine dining restaurants will have to showcase more of the natural world to stand out—we're going to have to be explorers. But we're also a fine dining restaurant. Fine dining restaurants are going to have to be much more specialized, and I welcome that. I think that's going to be so exciting. You see it in Japan right now: more focus on the ingredients, more focus on the season so that it isn't just pork and beef all year long—true diversity. It's something extraordinary that I think is going to happen much more in our region and the West in general, as well. Luckily it's more open now; there's not just one or two ways to set up a so-called fine dining restaurant anymore. For instance, at Noma we're vegetarian six months of the year.

Liz Benno, Lincoln Ristorante (New York): I would like to see fine dining not be bashed as much as it has been. It should be treated differently from casual dining, especially in the reviews. It's different, and it needs to be treated different. To have nine courses at Per Se, different for each person depending on which tasting menu they choose, be given two stars—the same as Superiority Burger... there's a huge difference. I think casual restaurants should be just as appreciated, just differently.

Skenes: Honestly, I would like to see better quality in America. I'm not even talking about the cooking; I'm just talking about the quality of the shit people are willing to serve, especially at the fancy places. You should be trying to get the best thing you can get, and not just picking up the phone and calling some dick who's going to deliver it in a truck from a warehouse around the corner. You should actually, really, in earnest, try to get real quality.

Let's just be clear, I'm also talking about myself. If I look back, I hate Saison from before. I hate everything about last year. I don't like anything other than right now, and in fact I hate that also, to be honest with you.

Before, we would buy stuff from Tsukiji, because it was the best thing we could get here. Finally, we just said, *Fuck it, we're going to do it:* pay fishermen to go out for us, pay their fuel, pay their labor, to get us these fish

> You're a chef in a fancy place—it's going to be difficult. If you don't like that, then do something else. This is a craft that is meant to be improved on a daily basis, and come on, if you're not doing that, you're just tricking people. —Joshua Skenes

alive—jellyfish, sea cucumber, shit that nobody was using at that time but we knew was there. The quality ended up being ten times better. You can ship something from Tsukiji but everything goes through transformation when you ship it. There are so many things that are beautiful and amazing, but our food systems are so fucked up in America—everybody just wants salmon. We need a real shift in thought, and we need to really follow nature and the seasons.

It's more difficult, yes. You're a fucking chef in a fucking fancy place—it's going to be difficult. If you don't like that, then do something else. This is a craft that is meant to be improved on a daily basis, and come on, if you're not doing that, you're just tricking people.

Anita Lo, Annisa (New York): I think things have to change. I think our industry is broken in many ways, but damn, it's incredibly hard. Everyone seems to be trying to do their fast-casual concept and a lot of these higher-end restaurants are closing—Bouley is closing—and it's very sad to see.

We can't find cooks anymore. The problem is money. I think New York has been the culinary center of North America on some level, but it can't continue the way it's going. We're losing restaurants. I find it outrageous that someone like Bill Telepan can't make it—he's a really great chef with a big name. They raised the minimum wage for waiters, and it crushed him. For a tiny little restaurant, that just doesn't make sense. I'm a liberal and I totally get why you need policy for places like Denny's. But is that really necessary for a high-end place where waiters are making decent money from tips?

We've tried out a no-tipping policy, and it hasn't been great. We've lost a lot of diners. I think people just don't get it—they have sticker shock and don't really get what it means.

Sandoval: I want to see more patience from chefs. I'd like to see cooks working under talented chefs longer than they are. I was twenty-six and an executive chef in Richmond. I shouldn't have been. I should have been working for someone else. I see others making that mistake. Once you're an executive chef at a restaurant and telling people what to do, your own learning slows down. The longer people wait to make that leap, the better they're going to be when the time comes. This is why it's so difficult to find cooks.

Is it important that young cooks spend time working in fine dining restaurants?

Shewry: If you look at all the successful young cooks in Australia—Dan Hong, Phil Wood, Dan Puskas, Josh Murphy, Aaron Turner, Analiese Gregory, all these young people on the rise—they've all had significant experience in fine dining restaurants. None of them, with the exception of Dan Puskas at Sixpenny, are doing something you could define as a traditional fine dining restaurant, but I guarantee they wouldn't be where they are if they hadn't spent the time in those kitchens.

Benno: I went to the French Culinary Institute in 1998. While I was there, fine dining was huge. Daniel Boulud came to the school to talk to us about doing externships—that's where I felt like I needed to be. I got the externship and it was really, really hard, because I was basically doing forty-plus hours of free work while going to school full time. Alex Lee was at Daniel when I was there, throwing garbage cans at people. I was basically cleaning mushrooms, watching service, and then getting all the mise en place for the cooks, and having them yell at me. It was crazy. I really didn't mind getting yelled at. It made me want to become a better cook, to work

I think it's important for cooks to work in a place where food is paramount and it's an exacting kitchen—and that can be rustic-exacting or more fancy-exacting—but it's got to have all the details, because it's really the details that make great food. —Anita Lo

In my generation, the chef was in the kitchen.
—André Soltner

dining isn't the food. It's their whole approach to things.

Kinch: It takes a certain individual to want to do fine dining. It's a lot of hours, a lot of information. The margin of error is much smaller, and expectations are much more demanding. Everything is, *How do we make it better?*

Benno: I loved my externship at Daniel, and it was a great learning experience. But I don't think it was where I wanted to be, though I still wanted to be on the higher end of dining. I didn't think I could handle a four-star French restaurant. I thought I needed to go a step down. I wanted to dedicate my life to cooking, but not 90 percent of it. I wanted to work at a really, really good restaurant, but I also wanted to take care of myself. I work to live, I don't live to work.

Crenn: Some people don't connect with fine dining; it doesn't make them less if they never work in fine dining. A cook is a cook.

Humm: When we have staff meal, there are some cooks who have a soulful approach to cooking and can cook anything and make it taste really good. And there are some cooks who've spent all their time in fine dining and are technically very good, but don't really cook from their heart as much. I'm really lucky that I grew up with a mother who's a great cook, so I sort of learned that soulful connection with food at an early

harder to not get yelled at. I actually appreciated it. One chef yelled at me so bad that foam was forming at the corners of his lips like a rabid dog. I never wanted that to happen again, because it's embarrassing. I feel like any cook should have that kind of experience and then do what they want to do.

Yannick Alléno, Pavillon Ledoyen (Paris): It's an education. I think it's a métier of gestures above all. To play piano or saxophone, you must work a lot. It doesn't come on its own. But you can come from anywhere; it doesn't matter. It's knowing where you're going.

Redzepi: For the most part, fine dining kitchens bring forth a high level of organization and work ethic, and they also train people to be very good craftsmen. Cooks go through one or two years, being in all the seasons, butchering, and doing all the hard work, and then many of them take that knowledge of flavor and organization and put it into an everyday environment. The way I see it, there used to be a lot of very bad everyday restaurants. The bar is higher now. I think the importance of fine

age—the connection to the farms, to washing greens and making a salad, and braising a piece of meat. If you didn't have that growing up, you can learn it in casual restaurants.

I do think working in fine dining as a cook is super important at some point in your career, but I also think working in a little restaurant, where everyone does everything and there are three cooks and you create beautiful meals with inexpensive ingredients, is also very important.

Sandoval: Working for a dynamic group of chefs—all different types—would be the smartest way to do it.

Kinch: I worked in a banquet kitchen at a hotel. God, I hated it. But it's important. There's a real art to feeding a lot of people in a short amount of time. I don't have much of an interest in it, but I'm glad that I did it.

Kostow: The lengths that we go to in our restaurant to educate our people, the amount we invest in our people, is bananas. A lot of this has to do with resources as much as anything, and it has to do with the kind of people that come into those environments. But do I think it's necessary to learn how to cook? No.

Lo: I don't think it's that important to work in fine dining. It depends on what you want to do in the long run. I think it's important for cooks to work in a place where food is paramount and it's an exacting kitchen—and that can be rustic-exacting or more fancy-exacting—but it's got to have all the details, because it's really the details that make great food.

Soltner: I did my apprenticeship in 1948. At this time, we did three years of apprenticeship, and from there, we went to work for one year at one restaurant, another year at another restaurant, and so on for a few years, until you could be a sous chef, and from sous chef to chef, and eventually to chef-owner. That's how I started. You have old timers like me who say apprenticeships are better—if we were in good restaurants we learned quite a lot, but we also did a lot of cheap work. Many times at our school, when I see what the students produce after six months, I know that I was not able to produce that after six months of apprenticeship. We learned by working, so we didn't learn as fast.

Alléno: I was a student of nouvelle cuisine. It was an era when you learned cooking with the habit of "Oui, chef!" The chef said something, you said yes, and you executed it. And therefore the reflex was one of boredom. The apprenticeship for this style of cooking was long. I was a good student of this cuisine, with its reflexes and its ways of doing things. It's good because the foundations are very strong, and with them you arrive at a "long-termist" creativity. It's also a very flavorful cuisine, one that couldn't survive today, because now everything is accessed through the image, and one often forgets one thing, and that's the taste.

What were your early experiences with fine dining, both as a diner and as a cook?

Crenn: I was eight or nine years old when I ate my first tasting menu, in Brittany. People's clothes were so well tailored, and it was black and white and ties and white gloves and everything was shiny and it was just so different from just walking into a bistro. I don't think I knew what I was experiencing, but I knew that it was different and for me, and it was just amazing.

Kinch: I was working in France, in a really traditional French restaurant that had one Michelin star, when I first had a meal click for me. I was twenty-three, and I knew everything. It was my first extended period in France, and I had just started eating at restaurants. I had only been to a couple three-star places. I went to this restaurant; it was called Alain Chapel…

The food was so bright and so simple and so delicious, yet so unlike anything I'd ever seen before. It was alien. There was a courtyard, and you sat underneath the trees underneath the veranda; there were birds in the fucking trees singing. It wasn't traditional, it wasn't classical—it was outside. It was innovative, but really, really simple. I think about that meal all the time—about how it made me feel. I

remember taking the train back home and realizing I knew nothing about food. I knew absolutely nothing.

Alléno: The first three-star I visited was Bernard Pacaud [at L'Ambroisie]. I ate a *feuilleté de truffe* with foie gras and truffle sauce—it was the era when the truffles had flavor. This was in 1992. Then I had lobster with red-wine sauce, in *civet,* with a purée of split peas. I didn't know that split peas could have such an exceptional flavor. Then I had lamb and a chocolate *tarte.* The second was Robuchon, when it was still in the 16th Arrondissement. It was the first time I had warm gelée, of foie gras. It incited me even more. I was a hotel chef—at that time, the hotels weren't like they are today; there weren't starred restaurants. We did our job well, but it wasn't our goal. When I had tasted this emulsion, that's when I thought, *This is what I want to do.*

Achatz: My very first experience was at Charlie Trotter's, in 1995. I was applying for a job there. Charlie said I could come in as a *stage* and try out. He made the tryouts cook a five-course meal for him and the sous chefs—there'd be a black box of ingredients and a set amount of time, and they'd say, "Ready, set, go." So immediately after Charlie invited me, I hung up the phone and booked

> I tell my guys this: If you're going to put yourself out there, you have to make sure that it's going to taste better—it's going to feel better—than going and getting a good burrito. Just saying it's fine dining isn't enough to create its value.
> —Christopher Kostow

> I would not be spending sixteen hours a day cooking for forty people if I didn't feel there was a greater purpose than just making these forty people happy. —René Redzepi

a reservation. I wanted to see what ingredients they were using in the kitchen, so I could think it through. I was twenty-one, a single diner, and nervous as hell. It was my first fine dining experience—I remember ordering two bottles of wine knowing I wouldn't drink any more than a glass or two, but I wanted them to know that I knew wine. And the meal was so magical. The elegance, professionalism, hospitality, it felt like you had stepped into somebody's made-up world. It was like being in a Harry Potter movie.

Shewry: I didn't grow up in a country with a system of judging restaurants with stars or numbers or hats. Now, there are so many different ways of finding out what the best restaurants are. But back then it was more word of mouth. When I first moved to Wellington from Taranaki, all the cooks used to whisper in hushed tones about this restaurant called the Roxburgh Bistro, about how incredible the chef was and how amazing the food was. They talked about it like it was some kind of pilgrimage to go there. I was maybe twenty-one, and I was pretty excited by that. My mother came down to stay with my wife, Natalia, and me, and she booked us dinner there. I went with my mother and wife, and after that point, it was real clear what super high quality was. I'd been cooking since I was fourteen, and I had never seen food like that—I'd never tasted food like that. I wanted to be a part of that, so a

few months later I applied for a *commis* position there.

Humm: When I was fourteen, I stopped going to school to become a professional cyclist—I was on the junior Swiss national team, I was sponsored, the whole thing. My dad, who was an architect, was totally against this idea. He said, "I'm not paying for any of this, you're on your own." And so I went on my off time and got a job in a kitchen and learned to cook. But when I was eighteen, I had a meal—ironically, it was for my father's birthday—at the restaurant of Frédy Girardet, who was one of the really great Swiss chefs with one of the best restaurants at that time.

We had dinner in the kitchen, which was super special. I saw these cooks with the toques and the way they moved around this kitchen and the way Girardet's voice was the only voice you could hear, and I could see how they were so concentrated and so focused, and it really blew me away. At that moment, I realized cooking could be competitive, that what they were doing was what I was doing on the bike all day long. I raced for a few more years afterward, but that moment was very, very big for me. When I decided to go full on into cooking, I wanted it to be with that intensity and precision.

I went to work for three-Michelin-star chef Gérard Rabaey at Le Pont

de Brent. In the five years I worked there, I got exactly what I wanted in the kitchen. It was amazing. Intense, focused, precise—it was just unbelievable. But in those five years, I never even saw the dining room. During service, Rabaey would pull down a glass window over the pass, leaving just enough room to pass your plates because he didn't want any communication between the kitchen and the dining room. No joke, the only way to communicate was with little notes with questions or answers on them. So fine dining was attractive to me, but only really for the kitchen side of things.

Sandoval: I was living in Richmond, Virginia, where I'm from. I moved out of my parents' house when I was sixteen, dropped out of high school, realized I needed to make some money, pay rent, and buy weed. So I started washing dishes at a place called Helen's Restaurant. For that time and for Richmond, it was the finest of fine dining places. I went from washing dishes to plating salads, and then developed a relationship with the chef, David Shannon. He said I should come in and dine at the restaurant as a customer. I was completely blown away. One of the first courses was littleneck clams with watercress consommé, Virginia ham, and some sort of bread crumbs. It was perfectly balanced, and I'd never had anything like it.

Kostow: I went to France, and the first place I worked was a one-star Relais & Châteaux where the food was a fraud. They'd buy beautiful *loup de mer* and freeze it all. At the beginning of summer, they bought all these pumpkins and then broke them down and froze them all to make soup. That totally changed my perception of the whole thing.

Later I worked at three-Michelin-stars in France, and I worked with Daniel Humm at Campton Place and it taught me a really big lesson. Just putting food in a pretty pile is not enough. I don't think your consumer now has the patience for the unnecessary pomp and circumstance. I tell my guys this: If you're going to put yourself out there, you have to make sure that it's going to taste better—it's going to feel better—than going and getting a good burrito. Just saying it's fine dining isn't enough to create its value.

Roellinger: Let's leave the world of the chef. One of the most important emotional moments I've had with food was with strawberries. I was going to pick them with my grandfather in the garden at eleven o'clock—the sun had begun to heat up the berries. There was still a bit of dirt on top of them, so we went to the water pump and turned it on all the way. There was quite a particular smell there, I know there were two or three frogs hanging around. The water was cool and we rinsed the hot strawberries, we cleaned them, and then we bit right into them. They were hot inside, but on the outside they were cool. For me, that was the first gustatory emotion that I remember.

Does the exclusivity of fine dining threaten its existence? Or does it create a necessary mystique?

Shewry: I don't think it's a threat. I was talking with one of my front-of-house staff the other day about whether or not we should block the front-door glass or leave it open. When people walk along the street, sometimes you'll see them peering in, wondering what's going on in the building. There needs to be a *What are they doing in there?* kind of feeling.

There's a part of me that knows that the cost of coming here—even though it is a good value—means that a lot of people in society can't come. In a way that's what fine dining means: it definitely excludes the majority of people in Australian society. That's a fact. But I don't feel like my idea of fine dining or Attica is elitist. Generally, restaurants of the ambitious nature are smaller. It's hard to get into the best restaurants in the world. There's a lot of exclusivity around that basic fact, not even bringing in the cost.

Alléno: I believe that fine dining can't be populist. A great restaurant is something luxurious, and the luxury, I believe, is earned. You must keep these parts of dreams so that a kid will want to be able to eat and drink great wines in a restaurant like that one day—it's a value in which everything is exceptional.

There are events where great chefs come to serve their food in cartons. I don't believe it's good. Fine dining should remain an environment, a smile, a greeting, a scent, a thickness of table, of crystal—it's part of things. In terms of food, most often our clients come to us and say, *Wow, I would never have been able to make this at home.*

Humm: I think it's a threat to fine dining. I really do. When I was young and cycling all over Europe, when I would

be in a town with a great restaurant, I would go by to see them, how they looked from the outside. Sometimes they had a menu outside and sometimes I could look through the windows. But I had such a fear of those restaurants, because I never felt like I could go in to eat and enjoy myself. And that huge, strange fear followed me, even after I'd worked in the best restaurants for so long. I was almost thirty years old before the terror started to fade. But I'd think to myself, *I don't have enough money. I don't wear the right clothes. I don't do this.*

We have to work hard to combat that, and the one hurdle that we cannot really remove is the price. This kind of dining is expensive. But everything else we try to overcome: we don't have a dress code, we have a bar where we allow walk-ins, and we offer à la carte dishes. We like when the bar gets a little loud sometimes, we like that energy in the room. Anyone is welcome, but it takes work on our part to try to make people understand that.

Lo: I think eating out is a privilege. On some level eating at all is a privilege.

Is fine dining exclusive? It's exclusive in that you have to be able to afford it. It's privileged, certainly, because a lot of people can't even afford to go out to dinner.

Is the question: Should fine dining not exist because it's expensive? I think it needs to exist. I think it's probably going to become more exclusive because of the current economic situation. But my mission here has always been about dialogue, about being able to sit down and talk, about bringing different cultures to the table. That message is not exclusive. I've tried my best to keep my prices low, to be the affordable fine dining, but it's almost impossible, especially now.

Skenes: There are expensive restaurants, restaurants that are medium-expensive, restaurants that are cheap, and whatever varying degrees in between. At each place, you should expect a certain level of quality, right? When you pay the prices you pay at Saison, then you should expect a fucking heap of caviar that's cured in salt that we harvested from seawater that we brought in, that we smoked and gave to our caviar packer, who aged it for three months. Everything is perfect about it, or as perfect as it can be at that time. You should expect that.

We have to accept that if you're going to cook really great food, it can't be on a really large scale. You can cook *good* food on a large scale—if you're going to do a casual chain you can still do it really well. I don't even like how big Saison is now, and the quality of the products we have here is as good or better than anywhere in the country. But for me, I still want better shit, because there is better shit that exists in the world.

Crenn: Sometimes I want to go and buy something from a designer that I like, and it's quite expensive. But I'm just so attracted to it and I love the designer. I'm not gonna buy that every day. There's also just go-to, no-brand clothing. It's also about finding that balance, how we can have two places. One will maybe play with their mind and their brain a little bit and maybe their taste also, but the other one is more familiar.

Kinch: I think there will always be a market for fine dining. It's that combination of innovation and people with the budget to support it. That's like asking if Dior is going to go out

of business, or if Ferrari is going to go out of business. Drive one. Drive one and appreciate what it is, the sensation it's creating that you don't even understand.

The older I've gotten, the more I appreciate the all-encompassing experience of going out to a restaurant. The service, the ambience, the food, of course, how you're treated, the welcome—is it genuine, is there eye contact? Then you get down to details, the quality of the bread, the water, the coffee, the butter on the table. Does that mean I don't like restaurants where you go and only care about the food? No, but you don't go to those places for your thirtieth birthday or your fortieth birthday, your fifteenth wedding anniversary, or whatever it is. There have to be restaurants that rise to the occasion, that grasp the gravitas of the situation.

Manresa doesn't feed two hundred and fifty people a night, we feed two hundred and fifty people a week. That's it. There are fifty people, scattered around the Bay Area at night, who understand what we offer and are willing to pay for it.

Alléno: Like art, gastronomy has always had a relation to the social evolutions of the time. When you look at China, there have been periods of fantastic glory. The arrival of communism meant that knowledge atrophied. It's coming back. You look at the great, great, great French age—it happened because the intellectuals gathered to eat and drink great wines. There is a real

relationship between well-being and the search for the absolute. And gastronomy is that in fact: the search for the absolute. That's why fine dining won't die, because there is nothing better. For example, the Chinese take great delight in great French wines. When the Chinese come to our restaurant, they come to drink the great wines, to have the beauty that we've had since 1840, in this *maison,* which was built in 1792. Could fine dining today find its place in a dark little street at the end of the *quartier*? I don't think so. Yes, it can happen, but if your wife, who's gotten out her jewelry, her beautiful dress, is stressing because she doesn't want this quirkiness in a difficult environment, it won't be the same pleasure. It's a whole.

How is the current economic atmosphere affecting fine dining?

Benno: I think after 2008, people are a little more conscious about money. *Why am I going to spend five to six hundred dollars on a meal when I can also get a really fantastic meal for thirteen dollars?* That's what's happening now; great restaurants are so

I believe that fine dining can't be populist. A great restaurant is something luxurious, and the luxury, I believe, is earned. —Yannick Alléno

much cheaper. You can get the same service, great service, and great food for cheaper.

Aizpitarte: Back in the day, many of the high-level restaurants worked at lunch like at dinner—especially in Paris and in bigger cities, but even in smaller towns—as they tried to follow their customers, especially business-men. Now they offer more affordable set menus, because people are no longer required to do business meet-ings in the grand fine dining restau-rants. Most people, I think, are much more open-minded now and, even for more important meals, go to more open-minded places. They already have said everything they need to say to each other on the Internet! But they still need to see each other.

Lo: I wouldn't recommend opening a restaurant, honestly. You do it only if you absolutely have to, because in order to succeed, it needs to be an obsession—you need to have that

kind of tenacity. It's not really worth it, especially right now in this eco-nomic climate. It's so much money. I've said that to people underneath me, to my offspring, as well, and it's great when they do and they succeed—I'm not anti-restaurant by any means—I just think that it takes a lot. If you really, really love it, then it can be great for you.

Crenn: It's an interesting question. When I opened Atelier Crenn, we were in a crisis here in San Francisco. We had a vision, and we kept push-ing for the vision, and we struggled a lot, until suddenly the tech came back to the city and it really changed the landscape of the city economically, for good and bad. Obviously, those people are looking for fine dining. They have disposable income and instead of going to a theater or to the symphony, they'd rather go to a res-taurant and eat and have an experi-ence. The new money is in their twen-ties—interesting people. A little bit annoying sometimes when they come with their phone and their iPad and things like that, but they are the new generation of wanting to go and try different things and are willing also to pay for it, which is great for us.

But we are blue-collar, and it sad-dens me that things are not balanced. And I'm concerned about it. Those are the cons of how the economy evolved here in San Francisco. I think San Francisco and the mayor should have

done something about it. Rent con-trol should've been everywhere. You can't take away the core of what a city is about. A city is about workers who work everywhere, and live here, not just some tech company that comes and goes. It's been hard for cooks to live in San Francisco. Working at a restaurant, you don't make a lot of money, and it's difficult.

Kinch: Everybody is invincible when the economy is strong. I mean, all these people are investing in restau-rants and going to restaurants right now. The last economic downturn? I mean, they were juniors in high school last time. I've seen the entire San Francisco restaurant scene flushed down the toilet twice in the past twenty-five years. It's going to happen again. San Francisco is a town with a restaurant for every seventeen people, and they continue to open restaurants. What's going to happen?

What continues to excite you about fine dining? What exasperates you?

Alléno: My favorite part is when it starts. The worst is when it's over.

Achatz: I like the social aspect of sitting at a table for long periods of time. I like the interaction with front of house, watching the ballet and choreography, the elements of the wine marrying with the food. I love the intentional aspect of fine dining.

In one word, freedom. That's why I'm drawn to it. That's why I run the business the way I do, because I feel like I have the freedom to decide whatever I want at the restaurant. —Ben Shewry

I like the planned elements, that someone is directing the show I'm sitting here and experiencing.

Crenn: What excites me about fine dining is meeting chefs who are cooking in a way that is very personal and doing things that no one's doing, and not following a cookbook or a stricture that has existed before. What I'm getting bored of sometimes is there's no soul on the plate, and it's just a machine.

I need to feel the chef's personality and how they think about food and also the emotion they bring through the way they cook. Not every dish is to my liking. But I appreciate the effort behind it and trying to understand what really made them go that far. Some people would be like, *Oh, god, why do you like this fine dining restaurant? It's not even food.* I'm like, *No, it is.* You have to take away what you know. That's very important because when you go out there, you have to leave your expectation and your egos, and really allow yourself to surround yourself with that experience. You're going to someone's house and she or he can showcase who they are as people. If you don't allow that, then you're not experiencing anything.

Kostow: What continues to excite me is the pressure and the idea of being the tip of the sword and trying to innovate, and, in some ways, trying to justify all of the accolades and attention. You wake up every day and say, *All right, how do we get better?* Very few people in any field have that. And that's exciting. The flip side is that the emotional math doesn't really pencil out, meaning what we put into it—our efforts, our stress, our time, the emotions and everything that goes into it—is not necessarily reciprocated by the understanding of the guest at all. I would imagine most chefs in my world probably feel the same. You walk out on a Saturday night and you wonder

sometimes, *Do they understand how beautiful that vegetable is?* Do they understand that nine people toiled in the field to grow that potato and that other people came in at six a.m. to make sure it was washed and someone else came in to cook the potato and so on and so forth? We have sixty people at the restaurant who spend their lives trying to make experiences for people, and I wish I could say that 100 percent of our guests understand that, appreciate that, but it's simply not the case.

Redzepi: I do like the commitment, and having the time to really go in-depth with the ingredients and products. Eating at the best restaurants can be some of the best experiences of your life that you will always cherish and remember. I really love to do that for people. When that happens and you feel you've done something special for people, it's the most gratifying thing.

But the spirit of fine dining came from the royal courts, and it still feels like it's been formulated with that aesthetic in mind, like you're dining with the upper echelon of the bourgeoisie. Of course, that's not how most people are comfortable, and there's a new standard for how to be comfortable today. Luxury today is about being comfortable. Yes, you still have to wear clothes, but you don't have to wear a specific kind of clothes to eat a delicious meal and sit for hours and talk with your wife while learning new things about food. You don't have to perform that ritual in that way anymore; places now have to allow people to be themselves and to be comfortable. If they don't do that, I think the fine dining establishment will die out.

Sandoval: Let's start with what pisses me off. I think aesthetics over taste is the worst thing right now. Making food look good is an art in itself, but food is food and it needs to taste good. There are a lot of filters on Instagram

to makes things look nice. What excites me? That there's more places opening. Having options to go out and eat. I feel like the fine dining community is coming back together after the last five to ten years on the decline.

Benno: I'm almost forty. Now I can't sit for four-plus hours eating. My stomach can't handle it, my brain can't handle it. I can't sit still. I get very antsy. I still appreciate it and love the hard work that goes into it, but I just can't.

Skenes: I really do enjoy and love going out to fine dining restaurants, I really do. I just don't like when you get somewhere, and the food is over-manipulated, and you can taste the fact that the whole line has touched your carrot, picked it up, blanched it in fucking water, put it in their pocket, put it in the fucking deli cup, left it there overnight, taken it out, forgotten it was on the counter for a couple hours, put it back in their pan, and then served it to you. It's fucked up. It just shouldn't be that way.

Here's what you do. You take that beautiful little carrot that just came out of the fucking ground—that poor fucking carrot, it's screaming. Just wipe that little thing down with a cloth and then peel it. Take those peelings, put that shit in a little carrot juice or a little chicken bouillon or a little vegetable bouillon. Maybe don't put it in anything. Maybe just brush it with a little butter that you made, because it's fucking so easy to make butter that's actually good instead of buying Plugrá from a fucking disgusting commodified feedlot, and then just grill it and serve it when it's cooked. See how simple that process is? Let's compare the two. Blanch it in water, shock it, put it in a deli cup, store it, pick it out, cook it again in some other way. Peel, cook, serve. I think there are some serious questions we have to ask ourselves as craftspeople in our profession.

Alléno: What excites me is the opportunity to prepare French cuisine of the twenty-first century, because the century's going to be very strange. Socially, it's going to be a very disturbed century, so we as cooks should prepare for that. It's going to be very different in ecological terms, social terms, etc. French cuisine should prepare itself for that. It's still really stuck on the codes of the nineteenth century.

Shewry: In one word: freedom. That's why I'm drawn to it. That's why I run the business the way I do, because I feel like I have the freedom to decide whatever I want at the restaurant. People come to see our expression of cooking and hospitality; they don't want to see another person's or another organization's expression.

Kinch: What makes me really excited about Manresa right now is that I don't have a lot of limitations on exploring things I want to explore, culinary-wise. Quality ingredients, technique, development of a new dish—I got nothing that really holds me back, logistically or from a financial standpoint.

What exasperates me, I hate to say it—it's not just in fine dining—are dietary restrictions, when people fine-tune menus to their own personal preferences. People who are afraid of food and feel that they need to dictate what we do. (Allergies, I completely understand.) I have a staff of thirty-six people, we feed fifty people a night, and we work long, hard days. Our entire individual and group focus is to create the best possible meal experience that the guests have. And yet, we have people come in and say,

I don't like red peppers and mushrooms, and they don't want to see it. It's not a restriction. They are dictating their concerns as opposed to allowing us to maybe open up their eyes a little. It's literally people who are afraid of food, and I find that exasperating. To me, that's not a good sign. You don't have to worry about the death of fine dining. You have to worry about the death of a certain kind of... hedonistic sensibilities.

I want people to come in and I want them to leave everything, including their cell phones, and their angst, and their anxieties, and their entire frantic outside world—that's what fine dining does. You're paying a lot of money—when you come into my restaurant, put the fucking phone away. Sit down and let us drive, and we're going to give you three hours, and when you leave it's going to feel like ten minutes.

Shewry: Another thing that fine dining affords me is some of the best young talent from all across Australia and the world. That is an amazing privilege. It's just a nice thing to be involved with passionate people all the time. It drives me, as well, because I have a responsibility to keep creating and doing new things for my team, as well. I feel exhilarated by that, but maybe I'm a bit of a psycho like that. I like the work. It's not hard work. It's massive fun. It's not a chore. Don't feel sorry for me.

Who are fine dining restaurants intended for?

Alléno: They're for everyone. When it interests you, you should be able to afford it. A year and a half ago, an eighteen-year-old couple came in. They were shy, a little frightened to be there. It's an impressive restaurant! It's up to us to understand, to feel, to put them at ease. We took care of them. They were so moved. They stayed more than four hours. They were interested, they were passionate. We could see they didn't have a lot of money. They had a little glass of wine. It was cute!

Sandoval: We're focused on getting people interested in food and wine, people who have an open mind, people who'll let us feed them. The ideal customer is trusting and willing to have a good time.

Crenn: Everyone. I think fine dining is intended for everyone. It's not a class thing, because people need space to celebrate. It's very important for someone to travel the world, and to find different experiences or understand different cultures, otherwise you're just narrow-minded. I remember this writer a long time ago was complaining about fine dining and how expensive it was, and it's like, *Why are you a writer?* To

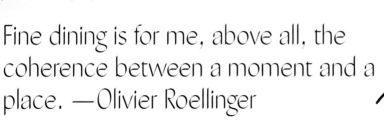

Fine dining is for me, above all, the coherence between a moment and a place. —Olivier Roellinger

> I want to give the guests a few things that are beautiful and nice and light and then send them on their way.
> —Nick Muncy

think: *It's just not worth it, worth my time, and this is wrong.* That's not the right way to think about things.

Shewry: It's meant for anybody who loves life, seriously. I know that sounds like a weird thing to say, but I'm a passionate person, and I always surround myself with other passionate people, and I'm hopeful that that positivity and that passionate attitude makes like-minded people want to come to Attica. We can gain so much energy from the positive exchange between humans when we get our job right.

Kostow: Anybody who craves a perfectly created experience and is willing to immerse themselves in that. We have people who come in who perhaps aren't that savvy, but man, when they have a good time, that's super rewarding. I don't know if there's a demographic I wish I would see more of, I just wish everybody would come in maybe less jaded, maybe get off their phones, maybe just understand that there are a lot of people working in the service of their experience. You've just gotta lift your head up and meet them halfway.

Kinch: I used to save my money for months to go have a meal in a great restaurant, because of what I learned and how it made me feel—excited. It's the cost of doing, the cost of education.

There are a lot of people who just have a lot of money, and spend it, of course. There are always going to be restaurants where rich people eat, and rich people who don't really care about food. There are always going to be restaurants and environments that cater to these people. But that shouldn't be the stereotype of what fine dining is. Nobody and nothing is perfect.

It's not easy being a pastry chef in fine dining. Dessert is both the last impression the restaurant will make, and something that must fit into someone else's tightly conceived vision. We spoke to two pastry chefs, a pastry-chef-turned-taquera, and the chef of a three-Michelin-star restaurant who has chosen not to have a pastry chef on his staff, about how the sweet stuff survives in a savory world.

How do you approach developing desserts for a fine dining setting?

Stephanie Prida, Manresa (Los Gatos, California): At the restaurant, dessert always comes after a huge tasting menu. I can't stuff this person full of pastry, as much as I want to. So instead we serve a first dessert and second dessert. First dessert is smaller, lighter, cleaner, with a kick of acid, and then second dessert is chocolate and one fruit dish, so if it's a two-top, each person gets a different dish, and if it's a four-top, there's two and two. Everyone gets something different.

Nick Muncy, Coi (San Francisco): It's different than dealing with a casual dessert menu where people want an ice cream, cake, and this and that all in one dessert, because they're only getting one thing. Here at Coi, I'll have one ice cream out of two or three desserts. I want to give the guests a few things that are beautiful and nice and light and then send them on their way.

My process has changed a little bit, because we were with Daniel Patterson and now it's Matt Kirkley as chef. With Daniel, there was no reusing ingredients and we had to keep everything local, so I would watch what stuff he was going to use for his menu, because I'd be getting whatever was left. (Whenever I'd put a new dessert on, the chefs would always jokingly say something like, *Ooh, raspberries sound good, maybe we'll take raspberries!* which would mean I'd have to change my menu.) Now we don't have the same limitations with keeping things local, because Kirkley's more concerned with getting in the best stuff. If there's something that's not grown here that he wants on the menu, we'll put it on—truffles, caviar, whatever. I just made a dessert with banana, and I'd never been able to use banana before.

How collaborative is the relationship between pastry chefs and head chefs?

Muncy: Daniel was more involved, especially in the beginning, because this was my first pastry chef job. I would work through dishes a lot with him. He's a very hard person to cook for and put dishes up to. He definitely knows what he's talking about and what he's doing. There'd be times where I'd give him the beginning of an idea, and if I didn't think he was really feeling it, I would just ditch it. I think it becomes difficult when you have someone trying to manage a vision in your head.

Kirkley wants me to figure things out on my own and go through my own creative process. I like to keep him in the loop and see if he has good ideas I wasn't thinking about. But really I'll just have Chef Matt taste it, and if he likes it, it goes on the menu.

I think the only thing that I've really changed is how I present the

stuff. I changed styles to match Kirkley's food, because it's important for the meal to look cohesive and not switch completely when the dessert courses come out. If I was still making dessert courses like I did with Daniel it would look weird, going from all this super meticulous food that Kirkley is doing back to natural plating. And Kirkley helped a lot with that kind of fine-tuning.

Prida: It all depends on the restaurant and the chef, to be honest with you. Sometimes it's a little bit of a fight because pastry is a way more narrow road, in terms of what product we can use. I'm really extremely lucky at Manresa. It's not like any other fine dining restaurant I've ever worked in. It's a very fair kitchen, and we're all very understanding of each other. Pastry usually has the makeshift den upstairs, where it's completely separated from the rest of the kitchen. It's not like that here. Pastry at Manresa is literally in the middle of the kitchen, so we're right there.

There really isn't a huge jump between savory and pastry. I think David Kinch has hired the same type of person to run both sides of the kitchen, people who have the same mind-set of what they think the food should be. We try to make it one cohesive menu, so that there's not

this idea for the guest of, *I'm done with savory, now I move on to pastry.*

Rosio Sanchez, Hija de Sanchez (Copenhagen): Pastry chefs like to be alone in their room—*don't touch my stuff, I'm gonna do this, it's my schedule, this is my pastry scale.* When I started doing pastry, I would do it alone at night when everybody was sleeping so I could be left alone, and then have people enjoy the pastries or whatever I made in the morning. A lot of pastry chefs are comfortable with that.

It was actually a little difficult in the beginning to work at Noma, because I was working with savory as well. It was just like, *This is how we work,* and savory chefs would come and help with plating, and it was a complete nightmare to me in the beginning. At Noma, we were a big team working on the menu. I adjusted to it, and I really like it now. I think it's just a matter of breaking down that wall—anyone can be trained.

When I started, Torsten Vildgaard and Søren Ledet worked on the savory, and I worked on the desserts.

When I started doing pastry, I would do it alone at night when everybody was sleeping so I could be left alone, and then have people enjoy the pastries or whatever I made in the morning. A lot of pastry chefs are comfortable with that. —Rosio Sanchez

There really isn't a huge jump between savory and pastry. —Stephanie Prida

It was attacked in a way like, *Potatoes are coming in season, Rosio. You should maybe try to work on a potato dessert.* And then people give some suggestions, there's a dialogue of where it should go, and then it's divided into who works on it.

The last couple of years that I was there it was totally different, because I moved into the test kitchen. That same process still happened, but it was more of a free-for-all. Some apples would come in and then me, Thomas, and Lars would start working on apples with no clear direction of where it was going. I was working on something that I thought was going to be an apple dessert—whole cooked apple, really nice and sweet and soft but still firm so you could kind of scoop into it— and René was like, *This is an appetizer.* In my head, I'm screaming, *No, it's a dessert!* But it was really liberating in that you don't have to confine yourself to something. I really enjoyed being able to work on something and figuring out what was the best for it.

It's super unusual. It's crazy. It's very hard to find a pastry person who is willing to make savory applications or even to take advice and critiques from savory chefs. I think having a lot of critique from savory chefs is a good thing, whether good or bad, because

a lot of desserts are way too sweet, they're too straightforward.

Joshua Skenes: For me, it's more cohesive not to have a pastry chef. A lot of chefs don't know how to make pastries, but if you do, then just make them yourself. The flow of the menu makes more sense. I think that there's a tendency with pastry chefs to over-complicate. When you put together a complicated pastry, where you have a base layer, a middle layer, a side layer, a garnish, a crumble, a streak, an ice cream, and some flowers, it's just not going to come together. Does it make sense to go from your main meat course—a simple broth made out of grilled bones—to some silly archi-tected shit? Focus on just a scoop of ice cream that's the single best-tasting and best-textured ice cream that exists, and you're gonna wind up with a much better product and a much better experience overall.

But there are lots of pastry chefs out there who would be able to do what I'm saying. If I had a pastry chef right now, it'd be fine, I'd be able to give them very clear parameters. Back when I had a pastry chef, everything was a hundred percent from the hip. Very little time was devoted to really sitting down and having a conversa-tion and taking a step back.

What are the specific difficulties you face in the pastry kitchen?

Muncy: You can sometimes tell when there's a savory chef doing desserts. They'll go to the same old tricks that everyone was doing ten

years ago, like a crumble and a torn up piece of cake with a quenelle of ice cream that doesn't look right. It's a little dated. A good pastry chef brings a lot to the meal: I'm doing fresh bread and well-thought-out desserts. I think it's important.

It's hard because people love des-serts, but given the option they'll be like, *I'm not that hungry. I'll be good today.* I feel like people only get des-serts here because it's part of the deal.

Sanchez: Not many restaurants can afford a pastry chef. And only maybe ten percent of people order dessert if it's not a tasting menu. When I started at wd~50 there was this huge pastry-chef boom in New York City. All these pastry chefs from these big restaurants were trying to make something happen, something cool. Johnny Iuzzini, Alex Stupak, Sam Mason, Dominique Ansel, Will Goldfarb were the major restaurant pastry chefs, and then they all left. But these restaurants still exist with pastry chefs—a lot of the chefs there just aren't really pushing to be in the magazines and spotlight. I don't think there's a lack of pastry chefs.

Prida: There is usually this idea that *I may skip pastry and do cheese.* It sucks because we work so hard and to have dessert be supplemental sucks. We can't control the guests and their opin-ions, but our job is just to make it as special and as interesting as possible.

For a savory chef there's no ending point—you can own your own restau-rant, be a chef forever, but in the end, there's nothing really in it for a fine dining pastry chef. I think it's hard for chefs to find the right pastry person, because there aren't very many of us. I think a lot of chefs don't have a pastry department because they just hav-en't found the right person. And after they've gone through so many people, they're like, *I'm not going to deal with this again.* LP

Inside Ledoyen

Photographs by Gabriele Stabile

Recently, while leafing through the July/August 1978 issue of WET: *The Magazine of Gourmet Bathing*, I came across a portfolio of double-page, full-bleed, black-and-white photos. There were pictures—big and back-to-back—with no words to get in the way of how the brain assembled what they meant. It seemed like a noble use of magazine real estate.

The text that preceded the portfolio explained that it was a temporary resurrection of the *Picture Newspaper,* formerly published out of New York City, mostly in the late sixties. Steve Lawrence, who started the *Picture Newspaper,* was quoted saying, "I was into what happens when images play off each other."

It was a magazine paying tribute to a newspaper. I thought, *Where are our picture pages? What about a quarterly paying tribute to a magazine paying tribute to a newspaper?*

So here's a portfolio of pictures from our longtime comrade in arms, Gabriele Stabile. He took them at Yannick Alléno's three-Michelin-star restaurant, Pavillon Ledoyen, in Paris. — PFM

Reign In

Interview by
Peter Meehan

Photographs by
Lyndon French

I interviewed the chef Iliana Regan over two days in the dining room of her almost-four-year-old restaurant, Elizabeth, located in an unmarked storefront on an unremarkable stretch of Western Avenue, in Chicago. Iliana is the chef-owner-bookkeeper-dishwasher of the place, which has a Michelin star and fans like René Redzepi.

When I arrived, she asked first if I wanted to "do anything," which led her to lend me a lethally sharp little knife so I could clean mushroom trimmings alongside a cook named Liz Parfitt for the better part of an hour. I tried not to cut myself as I joked with the folks in the kitchen, including Mikey Mudrick, who will be the chef of Iliana's forthcoming izakaya, Kitsune, and Justin Behlke, a chef who's friendly with the restaurant and sometimes hosts pop-ups there when it's closed for short development periods between menus.

Iliana had recently been named a Food & Wine *Best New Chef* and, in the weeks following that announcement, had closed a very short-lived but ebulliently celebrated spot called Bunny, The Micro Bakery. I was interested in her perspective on the restaurant game, how she got into it, and what she makes of what is going on in fine dining today. I started with a softball question, as one does.

You are a gay, alcoholic female chef in her midthirties cooking experimental fine dining food in a steakhouse city that likes its chefs white, male, and, when possible, handsome. What are you doing it for? Why?
A lot of times I feel like my answer is that it satisfies a creative need I have. And I guess when I look deeper down, for me it's absolute escapism.

I think it's the way that my brain is wired, and the way that I've lived life. How can I escape from living in this actual world? How do I get out of this body that I've always felt super weird and uncomfortable in? I'm awkward and I hate social interactions, but not

in the restaurant. This is the place where I feel most comfortable, my own little world.

This goes back forever, to books, where I spent a lot of time living.

What did you go to school for?
First I went to school for chemical engineering.

That doesn't seem very escapey.
I was good at chemistry and math, and where I grew up, you went to school to be a doctor or a lawyer. There were no creative things, people didn't really do that. Dads were insurance agents, and moms worked in that office.

About three years into school I decided to change majors, and I went to Columbia College and fell into a writing class, because it was an available elective. I really enjoyed it and went on to get my degree in it. But the whole time I was working in restaurants.

Where'd you grow up?
Northwest Indiana, in Hobart. At the time it was very rural; now if you go there it's more like urban sprawl.

When did you start cooking?
When I was fifteen and sixteen I would spend the summers with my sister, Elizabeth, and her husband in Georgia. She was much older than me—she was sixteen when I was born—and like a best friend-mother figure.

They had this old Victorian house with a garden in the back. I have these memories of sitting on that old wrap-around front porch in a hammock around sunset, and the music would be playing inside—she loved the Grateful Dead. She'd be drinking, because she always did. She was an alcoholic, but she was a really cool alcoholic. She would show up outside naked while cooking dinner with a spatula in her hand and say, *What are you doing out here? The bugs are gonna*

start biting, get inside! And it would seem unreal and weird, which was really cool to me.

And there were places in Georgia, in those older college towns, where you could walk into an old house that had become a restaurant. So I started to have fantasies that someday I'd have a house like that and a garden out back, and I would sell my fruits and vegetables in the front all day, and then I would invite people who stopped at the roadside stand for dinner in the evening. That was my first concept, back when I was fifteen or sixteen. I would tell my friends, "I'm gonna go to school for a science degree, but someday, this is what I'm gonna do."

Back in Indiana, my secret girlfriend at the time and I would steal money from her dad's wallet and drive to Michigan City because there was this French restaurant that was just off the shore. They'd bring out bread with roasted garlic and olive oil, and they had fresh berries with crème anglaise for dessert, and little chickens. It was completely, *Whoa, this is awesome*. That was my first exposure to French cuisine or French country cooking. Looking back, I don't know how real it was, but it blew my mind at the time.

My first job in the back of the house was at a French-country-cooking-style restaurant, learning quiches and crepes and sauce-making, soups, lots of stews. I picked up some fundamentals, quick breads and basics, traditional cooking, but not anything terribly advanced. My first taste of real fine dining came later, when I was going to school for fiction writing. I got a job working at Trio, in Evanston, back when Grant Achatz was the chef.

Those guys were *chefs*. It wasn't like a chef with a bunch of people who did prep work, it was all these chefs who went to school to be chefs, and everybody was very serious about being chefs. I saw the

Zucchini with hollandaise and flowers and greens from Regan's garden. The zucchini is dried and then rehydrated in carrot oil, buttermilk, lemon juice, and chicken fat.

You saw that cooking could be narrative. Where did you go from Trio?

My sister Elizabeth died, so I left Trio and I went back to one of the lobster-with-parsley-on-the-plate places. I needed time to collect myself, because everything was a mess, and by then I was an alcoholic and cocaine addict myself, so that was a much easier job, and I could hide in that and be as crazy as I wanted to be. And then pretty much from the time I was twenty-one until I was twenty-seven, I worked front of the house while I was finishing college because of the hours and, frankly, the pay. It's something that I regret sometimes.

After a year away, I went back to Trio because I really missed a more structured environment. When Grant left, I wasn't asked to go to Alinea, so I figured I had better stay put because I was in college. But eventually, I started to hit up Grant and Joe Catterson, saying I really want to come over to Alinea. After my noncompete at Trio was over—about two years after Alinea opened—I started there, a month before Grant was diagnosed with cancer.

And were you sober by that point?

No, that was 2007 and I didn't get sober until 2009. From the time I was twenty-two, I had gone in and out of AA trying to get sober or stay dry. But it wasn't until 2009 that I actually quit. Nothing bad happened at that time, really. I mean, I definitely put myself in precarious situations. I have woken up in jail cells not knowing how I got there. All kinds of dumb shit. Woken up with somebody in my bed who I was like, *Oh, I actually hate you at work, why are you here?* All these situations I didn't want to be in, situations that would probably make a normal person think, *Yeah, I should stop drinking.*

About a year into my job in the front of the house at Alinea, I thought, *I'm twenty-eight years old, I need to stop*

creativity and the way that Grant's food was, and I really related to that and thought, *That's the way I want to be with my writing.*

What is the difference between what you saw Achatz doing and what was happening at that French-country-cooking restaurant?

For me, it was the dedication and the belief in it. We would have meetings about how we would serve dishes to the table: how to set them down, how to be aware of our presence around the guests.

I started as a reservationist to get my foot in the door, and then I quickly moved on to different positions and ended up as an expediter—essentially working in the kitchen but not as a chef, running the flow back and forth.

That had a huge appeal, the fact that there was so much that was going into a dining experience. And seeing the actual stories that the food was telling—because Grant *was* telling stories with the food. He'd say, "We put pine in the bowl because that's like when my dad and I would go hunting in Michigan." And that definitely appealed to me, especially at the time, as I was changing careers and going to school for writing. So as I got more into my writing education, I thought more and more about the dedication that they were putting into their cuisine. Eventually I started to wonder, *Can chocolate be clear?* Or, *I wonder if this ingredient would go with that ingredient?* I'd start to develop menus in my head. At that time, that sort of cuisine was super mystical.

waiting for something big to happen for me to open my own place, I just need to do it. So I started a food company called One Sister. I was growing herbs, flowers, and vegetables in a little garden at my dad's house in Crown Point, Indiana. I would take them to farmers' markets and prepare them into products I could sell. I'd get off work at one in the morning at Alinea, and then at four o'clock in the morning start driving down to Indiana to get to the farmers' markets. I started making pierogi and they were the real hit. People in Chicago started writing about them, and I built a little bit of a name based on that.

I left Alinea in July of 2008 and started splitting my time working front of the house for my friend Tony Priolo's Italian restaurant, Piccolo Sogno, doing the farmers' markets, and *staging* at restaurants on my days off. I called up Michael Carlson at Schwa and told him I needed to work on my continuing education. Michael and I used to party together, and his sous chef at the time, Nathan Klingbail, was one of my really good friends from Trio.

I formed my own curriculum to teach myself how to cook in a more modernist way. I had no idea how to do it beyond hearing people say, "Oh, we put Ultra-Tex in this to thicken it" or "We made jelly with agar." I would go around to different restaurants and stage and ask a lot of questions. Michael let me order hydrocolloids through his restaurants, and I took them home and started practicing.

Eventually I started to write out those menus that I had been thinking about over the years, and called some press that I had gotten to know while doing the pierogi business and said, "Hey, I'm gonna do this underground dinner thing, are you guys interested in writing about it?" It actually booked me up for a whole summer, even though I think the food at the time was based on a lot of trial and error.

But my trials got better, and I was proud of it. People seemed to like it, because they kept coming. I called Henry Adaniya from Trio and asked him for advice on investors. He said, "Never take less than 51 percent of your own company—and they need to understand that you're not gonna make them money. If you can find the people that are willing to invest in you as an artist, then there you go."

I found three people who invested $150,000 together, and I had the seed for what I needed to launch Elizabeth. It wasn't a lot of money, but I had Michael Carlson as an inspiration, so I knew it wasn't impossible to open a fine dining restaurant and tell a food story with a really low budget.

You found money. How hard was it to find cooks? There's a lot of kvetching about the quality of cooks these days.
I think that there are good cooks out there—and I don't think that they all expect things to be handed to them. It's a matter of finding them and being willing to teach them.

I absolutely approach my job from the standpoint of being a teacher, but I need students who are ambitious and willing to work. I tell everybody who comes in here, "I am not gonna chase you around, I'm not gonna breathe down your neck, and I'm not gonna berate you. But I will know if you're not living up to what I expect, and you'll weed yourself out."

As we've become established as a restaurant, people seek us out and know what they might be getting into, rather than blankly coming in because they need a job or they want to be at a Michelin-starred restaurant.

Of course some kitchens are super brutal, and I've seen that firsthand. Sometimes women in those kitchens are avoided or ignored—I think it's because chefs have a hard time adapting their management style. It was like, *I don't know how to not yell at this person, but if I yell they'll cry, so I'm not gonna interact at all.*

How many boys know how to talk to girls at all, much less in a respectful way?
I had a girl who had worked at a great restaurant in the city and she said most of the time it was okay, but occasionally there were comments like, "Oh, you guys overthink things"—"you guys" being females. Or if passes that were made by certain people weren't taken in the way that they wanted them to be taken, then you were treated like garbage.

I very quickly trained her, and she was really freaking good. I actually learned a lot from her in return. She was only out of cooking school for maybe a year and a half by the time

she came to me, but there are blind spots in my knowledge because I didn't have a culinary-school education. There were things she knew from school that I hadn't taught myself or picked up in any of the kitchens I had been in. I know that if I keep my eyes open, there's a lot I can learn from the people that come through my restaurants, whether they are well trained or interns.

Elizabeth is not, to my mind, an overly traditional fine dining restaurant. It's small, it's handmade, it's intimate—but you have a Michelin star, you have some degree of national and international attention. How do you relate to the larger fine dining world?
I recently went to dinner at Oriole and it was fantastic. Everything was beautiful and pristine, and the food and the technique were great—all the things you'd expect at a tasting-menu restaurant. Watching the service and the flow on the floor was a pleasure—there was the front waiter and the captain and the back waiter and this whole system.

We would love to have a formal service here, but I don't have the means. Last night I was talking to my sommelier—who's also the captain who's also the floor manager—about how we can improve service without it seeming stuffy. My cooks are the food runners, I have one sommelier, one guy who polishes the glassware and is also the bartender, and one front waiter. The chefs all rotate through the dish pit, including myself—we don't have a dishwasher. At three and a half years old, we haven't really formalized a system, because we've always had to change it depending on our finances. It's burdensome.

Switching gears, then, what makes you happiest?
Writing menus and testing them out. When an idea comes to me and I get

to figure out how it should look and how to put it together and develop the recipe. It's very much like the writing process for me. It's telling a story in that arcing way, figuring out how we are represented, and, if we're cooking along a theme—like *Game of Thrones* or Native American—how we are tying the food to the narrative.

Are the themes an essential part of the storytelling? Or a crutch?
The themes are a big part of our success, and people love it. I'd rather cook whatever came into my head each day. I would like people to come to the restaurant for that rather than the theme because it actually *is* that, only with the narrative tied in. So it does feel like part of it is a bit of a compromise, and that can sometimes be a little bit ego-crushing. But I've made so many sacrifices for this business, and I will do whatever it takes to serve people our food.

Do you take it personally that it's hard to get twenty people to pay $105 a night?
I don't anymore. I think there were times when I did, and I don't think I even vocalized it or expressed it. We treat everybody kindly who comes through the doors. Do I have dark thoughts? Yes. But I think that's also part of my alcoholism—my brain will go to the worst possible scenario all the time. I have this weird paranoia about a lot of things; it's like being an egomaniac in reverse—I assume that you hate me, but it's not about me at all; you're having a bad day. So I try to think that same way about my client base or the food.

All I know is that I keep trying to put out the best food I can, and if people aren't coming, I can't take it personally. But really it's about perspective, because we are full just about every night. We are currently booked out until August. I know from my own experience that we're a good

restaurant, plus there are outside factors like *Food & Wine* and Michelin that say we're good. Are we the best? No. Are we second-best? No, absolutely not. We play around a lot and do a lot of experimentation, and sometimes I think, *Maybe I should have cooked that meat differently*. I think that's also part of the free market of having this little place: I get to do some things and fuck up, experiment all I want.

This is my livelihood and, frankly, I enjoy it. I'm creating the menu and then teaching it and doing the R&D, and then I've gotta do the payroll and write out the checks and monitor the bank account and pay the sales taxes and deal with this person who's got a complaint about the dishes. I'm all hands-on, doing everything, managing every aspect. If I'm broke and I still want to order truffles, I can do it, and the only person beating me up for my food costs is myself.

How do you feel about that bargain, that exchange?
Some days I hate it. The other day I was in the office and I was writing out the insurance check and Liz, my sous, wandered in and I told her, "Don't ever open a restaurant. Get a really sweet head-chef job at one of the international hotels where you can go live in France for a year, maybe go live in Hawaii or Bermuda."

I think if I had to redo things, maybe I'd test those waters. My friend asked me recently if I'd ever thought about working with a big restaurant group, where all I'd have to do is be the chef. Sometimes that idea does appeal to me, but it comes down to control. She asked me if I knew this famous Milton quote— "Better to reign in Hell than serve in Heaven"—and I was like, *Yeah, that's totally me*. There are those days when I think, *Fuck this business*. But I do get to do whatever the hell I want here, and most of the time I love it. ◼

COREY LEE'S

COLLECTION OF

MASTERPIECES

BY

TIENLON HO

PHOTOS BY

ERIC WOLFINGER

Corey Lee will tell you that his goal in opening In Situ—the flagship restaurant inside the San Francisco Museum of Modern Art—was never to open a restaurant at all.

Following a three-year, $610 million expansion, SFMOMA is now one of the largest collections of modern and contemporary art in the world. In 2014, the museum directors tapped Lee to fill its ground-floor dining space with something fitting. For Lee, the dining experience had to be more than a café version of his other San Francisco restaurants, Benu and Monsieur Benjamin.

What he created instead, housed in both a walk-ins-only lounge and a more formal dining room, is a rotating collection of dishes from chefs around the world, a gallery of dishes of today and days past, replicated as faithfully as possible. Instead of a restaurant with a singular vision, it is a constant collaboration. Instead of a menu, a catalog of great works. Diners order à la carte, making it possible to taste dishes that would otherwise require dedicating an entire evening to a tasting menu, a trip to a remote countryside, or at least the favor of a reservationist.

But Lee will tell you that In Situ is not just for people who couldn't get a table at Noma or Mugaritz. "Even if you stumbled upon this restaurant and never heard of any of these chefs before, I wanted it to be about the greater experience of connecting with these cuisines, understanding the nature and power of food," he said. In Situ breaks down the barriers between diners and the upper echelons of cooking without watering down the food. "Historically, access to this kind of cooking, which takes so much time, skill, and energy, was reserved for those with extraordinary means," explains Lee. "Today, things haven't changed so much, except now people who might never make a reservation at these restaurants will buy the cookbooks and follow the chefs on social media. It was important to give more people an opportunity to actually try this food—not just look at photographs, but to actually experience it for themselves."

Planning menus built off other people's dishes defies restaurant culture. For one, chefs can be fiercely protective of their work. And those who built their names on the uniqueness of their local ingredients don't exactly love the idea of exporting it from its geographic context, either. Is it still your food if both you and your terroir are out of the picture? It's probably why no one has done this before.

When Lee first proposed the idea, no one from the museum balked (perhaps because he didn't mention outright that they would have to build him a kitchen equipped to handle every cuisine on the planet). But even more surprisingly, no one from the chef community hesitated, either. Lee e-mailed and met with one hundred and ten admitted control freaks, asking them to share their recipes with his kitchen. David Chang, Nathan Myhrvold, and René Redzepi were the first ones in.

COREY LEE: There was almost no convincing to be done, because there was history there, years of knowing each other or maybe having our cooks work in one another's kitchens. Even with those I've never met, as chefs, we already spoke the same language. There were only a few I never heard back from.

ROY CHOI: We have a kung-fu code as chefs. There are certain people we trust, certain masters who have earned our confidence to carry on messages for us. That comes from years of not currying favor, and letting your work speak for itself. There are maybe a few others like Corey—Redzepi, Adrià, Passard, Dufresne—true sages of our industry. If they're calling you, they've thought a lot about it. That's how Corey got the license from all of us. That, and the folklore is that the guy can see an eyelash on a plate from two hundred yards away.

MATT ORLANDO: This project was Corey's way of connecting with

ne. He is extremely humble
s a tremendous amount of
t for other chefs. I think it was
o all of us that this was his way
ng respects, to give everyone a
e to shine.

ame In Situ means "in its orig-
osition or place." In art, *in situ*
o works created specially for
cular space—a gallery wall, a
obby, a tech start-up's bathroom.
er, many dishes coming from
places would create something
y different here, an original
ence in this new place.
nuseum at its best brings people
er, shows us where we came
nd offers a glimpse at where
eaded. It's a place to find
t and common threads as much
a forum for debate. Lee thinks
taurant at a museum should do
ne. A meal here might reveal

the origins of the Spanish avant-
garde, the connections between
Japanese *kaiseki* and French nouvelle
cuisine, how chefs from Hong Kong
to Los Gatos use sea urchin in utterly
different ways, and most importantly,
how all of these far-flung chefs influence one another.

LEE: We focused on chefs who were
trying to do something more than
cook delicious food. We looked for the
dishes that start a dialogue or tap into
an emotion.

For many years, I thought of
cooking as more craft than art. It's
something you do with your hands,
and it requires repetition. But now I
think food can be art in that it can be
a medium for complex expression.

When you look at classical art,
a portrait or a landscape, you can
immediately appreciate if it's realistic
or pretty. But with modern art, it's

not always so accessible. The ability
to fully appreciate a work comes
with knowing what's behind it. As a
modern chef, I'm also trying to touch
on something besides the immediacy
of taste. The goal is to make food
that reflects and informs how we live
our lives.

To fully understand each chef's
dish, Lee and his executive chef,
Brandon Rodgers, delved deeper than
the written recipes and notes each
chef shared. Lee cooked on the line
with Tanya Holland at Brown Sugar
Kitchen in Oakland and studied
videos Daniel Boulud sent demon-
strating Black Tie Sea Scallops, a dish
of layered scallops and truffles *en
croûte* that he created in 1986 at
Le Cirque in New York. Gastón
Acurio's executive chef, Victoriano
Lopez, made *cebiche* at the San
Francisco outpost of La Mar. Seiji

Yamamoto e-mailed a forty-three-page instruction manual for the *wagyu* sukiyaki he created at Nihonryori RyuGin, in Tokyo.

There were also field trips around Asia, the U.S., and Europe. In Osaka, Hajime Yoneda, of the restaurant Hajime, showed Lee how to prepare a dish called *ame*, the Sound of Rain. When the citrus granita is plated with liquid nitrogen on a lotus leaf, the plate begins to mist, and hidden gas-charged pellets beneath patter like raindrops. Hajime explained that the dish was meant to evoke the emotion of the sadness of a rainy day, but the pleasure of eating it echoes the duality of every moment.

Lee realized that in order to recreate the dish in San Francisco, there would have to be some substitutions—instead of lotus, they would use nasturtium, a modification Hajime approved. But wherever possible, Lee seeks to replicate complete details. Shipments arrived of porcelain plates for Peter Goossens's (Hof van Cleve in Belgium) salmon *tataki*; hand-thrown bowls for Cassidee Dabney's (The Barn at Blackberry Farm in Walland, Tennessee) slow-cooked egg; and baskets by the same weavers in Hastings that Isaac McHale employs for buttermilk fried chicken at the Clove Club in London. Lee assured each chef he would go to whatever lengths were required to do right by their dishes, and they did the same. In the spring, when Lee couldn't find tomatoes that would cut it for Torre del Saracino's (Vico Equense, Italy) *spaghetti al pomodoro*, chef Gennaro Esposito shipped over a pallet of tomatoes he had tinned himself.

LEE: This all happened through continuous, open communication. A chef explaining how to make a dish is much different from reading a recipe in a book. Because they knew that I was actually going to cook and serve their dishes, we talked about the variables, the sourcing, which part of the ingredients to use—all those little details that you explain to one of your own cooks.

When Lee and Rodgers flew to Charleston to see Sean Brock at McCrady's, his master class on brown-oyster stew with benne included a contextual trip to Hannibal's Kitchen, Brock's personal soul-food mecca, for lima bean and pork neck stew.

SEAN BROCK: Brown-oyster stew is steeped in the Gullah/Geechee culture along the Carolina coast. When I started messing with this dish in 2009, I was just trying to understand this very historic thing. It's a traditional West African dish brought by slaves that made its way to the Big House. It proves the West African contributions to Low Country cuisine are so fundamental. This is a touchy subject now, and rightfully so. This is a part of culture that we're ashamed of. So when we serve this stew, it opens up a dialogue about culture and civil rights. We end up talking about more than deliciousness, and that's good for everyone.

Choi's dish is Ketchup Fried Rice, a bowl of rice and vegetables seasoned with ketchup and topped with a fried egg, a recipe he has never cooked in a restaurant but shared in his book *L.A. Son.*

CHOI: When my family got to America, there were no Asian markets. You had to be creative translating what you grew up with into ingredients you could find or afford. Ketchup was a luxury. I wouldn't have chosen this dish for any other chef to pull off but Corey. He ate this as a kid, too, so I knew he'd get it. It's a dish of a chef who grew up in LA in a Korean family, who has a French foundation but also ate stuff straight from the can. I wanted to have someone sitting in this museum stop and say, "What the fuck? Who is this, and why did they do this?"

For at least one other chef, the project was a chance to speak. Anthony Myint decided that his dish at In Situ would visually represent the environmental impact of what we eat. The result was the Apocalypse Burger, a beef patty encased in a crisp shell of squid-ink-blackened flour and edible clay, puffed in oil like Indian puri. The result resembles a charcoal briquette. It's as much a striking trompe l'oeil as an edible metaphor (broadly speaking, food production accounts for about half of greenhouse-gas emissions, with feedlot beef being a top emitter). Myint sent Lee photos and three pages of detailed notes, knowing full well that his recipe had so far yielded a picture-perfect result only half the time.

ANTHONY MYINT: Corey sent back a picture of the recipe testing, saying, "It's not bad. I'm getting 95 percent yield." That's who he is. Give him an imperfect thing and he can make it nearly perfect.

Cecilia Chiang, who introduced Americans to the concept of Chinese fine dining with the Mandarin, in 1961, has shared many conversations with Lee through the years about the disappearing authenticity in Chinese restaurants. Lee requested her recipe for *guo tie*—northern Chinese-style pork pot stickers—promising to make them correctly. Lee made multiple trips to Chiang's house for taste testing, learning to cook them *sheng jian,* steaming and lightly frying simultaneously in the pan.

CECILIA CHIANG: It is not easy to cook in all these styles, nor is it an easy job to work off of someone else's recipes.

That takes a lot of concentration and time, trying again and again, tasting and asking the original chef, *What do you think of this? Is that okay now?*

DANIEL PATTERSON: Even in the kitchen where the dishes origi-nated, it's not going to be perfectly consistent every day. To replicate a dish is incredibly difficult. You pick up a Jasper Johns painting and move it around the world, it's still going to be the exact same painting. In cooking, your ingredients are different every day, the weather is hotter, or you might just be in a different mood. As Instagram will tell you, it's easy to copy the form of something, but it's really, really hard to copy the soul of something. And I think that's what Corey's trying to do, and do it at a very high level. I don't know of anyone who's done this before—not with attri-bution, anyway.

If you ask Lee, the most difficult dish to replicate came from Nahm, David Thompson's restaurant in Bangkok.

LEE: I had to go there. That alone was no joke, and when I arrived, they showed me seven dishes in one after-noon. I'm not well versed in Thai

food, so I wasn't just learning a new dish, I was learning a new cuisine and language at the same time. They were naming technique after technique and showing me fruits and vegetables I'd never even seen. I can't remember my kitchen IQ ever being as low as in that kitchen.

DAVID THOMPSON: Thai food is notori-ously complicated. If you're uncertain about it, it's a culinary minefield from which very few come out unscathed—diner or cook. Other major chefs have come and been equally at sea. Frankly, when I'm in a European kitchen, I'm baffled, because I haven't cooked it in a long time.

LEE: David was like, *I don't think this is possible,* and I was like, *You could've told me this before I came to Thailand.*

THOMPSON: Eventually he decided on *larb*—a mix of guinea fowl, red shal-lots, mint, the obligatory chilies, and lots of fresh vegetables and herbs. It is full of flavor and requires skill but is not as fraught as other dishes we considered. Corey got along terribly well with Prin Polsuk, the head chef, and he chose this dish for Prin, too, because it represents the distinc-tive flavor of northern Thai cooking, Prin's home region.

LEE: So this is where it gets crazy. Prin went to Chiang Mai and got them to put together a huge batch of this spice mix, brought it back to Bangkok and gave it to Andy Ricker (chef of the Pok Pok restaurants in Portland, LA, and New York), who put it in his luggage and flew to LA and then shipped it to us. So now we have a stockpile of this spice mix.

THOMPSON: *Naam phrik laap* is a blend of at least a dozen dried spices—Sichuan peppercorn, *makh-waen* (prickly ash), long pepper, galangal, chili, black pepper, white

pepper, and so on. If you eat a disproportionate amount of the spice mix, you're in for a bit of a shock the next day.

LEE: I'm acutely aware of how big of a responsibility I have to these chefs, and how much they're entrusting me to represent them. There are many things to be cautious about with this project, but most importantly, not letting anyone participating down. That's why we're being as faithful as we have the ability to be, in terms of ingredients and products and our abilities to replicate. It's not just doing one event or a talk together. This is an event where you continue representing them.

ORLANDO: Part of the excitement is that you'll never recreate a dish identically no matter what, no matter how many recipes and pictures you have.

The products are different. That's the exciting part, to see what comes out, and to see how it comes out in someone else's hands. Who knows? Maybe it'll be even better.

A CONVERSATION ABOUT A SUMMERY WARM TOMATO & BASIL TART
Corey Lee and Michel Guérard talk through how they crossed eras and oceans to recreate a dish from Guérard's restaurant, Les Prés d'Eugénie.

LEE: Michel Guérard is one of the great chefs of nouvelle cuisine.

GUÉRARD: Nouvelle cuisine was a reaction against immobility. Most chefs were still cooking under Escoffier, a great chef no doubt, but some wanted more creativity. It was popularized as a movement by journalists in the seventies, but the principles were there in the seventeenth century. We just led a gentle revolution to allow French cuisine to evolve and transform.

LEE: He was one of the first chefs anywhere in the world that I really looked up to and was inspired by. I first read about him in the book *Great Chefs of France*. I was probably eighteen or nineteen, and was just getting my first real turn at cooking, cold-calling kitchens around England. That book was my first look into the French world of haute cuisine, Michelin stars, and that caliber of chefs. What I still remember clearly is a picture of Guérard dressed like a woman, resting his head on Paul Bocuse's belly as they danced. That revealed so much about his personality.

GUÉRARD: Ah, that photo was taken at an event Bocuse organized at his restaurant in Lyon. Paul was dressed as a corsair, and I was a young lady. Paul is taller than me, so I was leaning my head on his chest, and we were holding hands, dancing slow. We were having fun. That photo captured the nature of our friendship, our mutual respect. It was the height of nouvelle cuisine and an extraordinary time of our lives. We were joyous and working hard. We really lived!

LEE: After looking up to him for three decades, witnessing him rewrite French gastronomy, I never thought we'd someday collaborate. I still get starry-eyed that this has happened. I realize now, without this project, I never would have been able to carve out the time to learn from him at this level.

GUÉRARD: When Corey contacted me, I hadn't heard of a project like this before, anywhere. There are restaurants in museums, but none do it this way. Sometimes ideas just come like a firework. I jumped in blindly, just knowing his reputation as a consummate professional. Three Michelin stars are a bit like a passport.

I chose this dish for Corey because it conveys the simplicity I pursue in all my cooking. The ingredients are at the core. It is at once rustic and elegant. Just because a dish is simple does not mean anyone can make it.

I sent a step-by-step recipe, which I thought would be no problem for a professional to follow. A well-trained, skilled chef understands the principles of fine cuisine. From our interactions that followed, it was clear he had the sensibility necessary to execute this kind of recipe and that he understood it at a profound depth.

It comes from a memory of my grandmother in the orchard in Vétheuil, a village on the bank of the Seine. She was the first great chef that I knew. We would harvest the fruits at their peak. All the secrets of her cooking were there in their ripeness. She would arrange the fruit in a circle on the crust with some butter and sugar, and pop it in a wood-fired oven. It was simply marvelous.

I make the *feuilleté*, layered pastry, with about the same technique that she used. Mine, I would say, is a little lighter. (I hope my grandmother is not offended!) You must use only just enough flour, not a speck more.

LEE: When executing any dish that is seemingly simple, with just a few ingredients, every little step and gram counts.

GUÉRARD: Above all, this recipe depends on the tomatoes. They must be very sweet and bright, dense and plump, like the ladies in old paintings. You cut them into rondelles, remove the water and seeds, then place them on the pastry with a reduced concentrate of tomato if it needs it, and bake at full blast. When you take the dish out of the oven, you glaze it with pesto—olive oi and basil—to bring in flavor and make the tomato glisten. You must eat it right out of the oven, still warm and crunchy.

LEE: I've been concerned about the ripeness of the tomatoes we've been getting in California. All the tomatoes in this dish are cooked—either baked or simmered down as a compote. So it's not just underripe tomatoes that would be an issue—over-ripeness would change the dish. Texturally and flavor-wise, they need to be just right. If they aren't, we'll have to wait to put this on the menu.

GUÉRARD: There would be no haute cuisine and gastronomy without humility toward natural ingredients. Cooking this way is entirely about allowing people to taste ingredients as they are, unadulterated. A great chef knows not only how to treat the ingredient but to express its essence. You cannot pretend the ingredient is your slave. This understanding shows Corey is a true chef. **LP**

The Idols of Fine Dining

by Aralyn Beaumont   Illustrations by Armando Veve

Within each culinary era, there are certain dishes that exemplify the zeitgeist and others that bend the course of cooking in a new direction. What follows is a list of thirty such iconic dishes, selected from the past century and a half of fine dining. We see these dishes recreated again and again in different forms by chefs who admire and take inspiration from them.

It is by no means a definitive list. It may seem disproportionally French, because it is: much of modern fine dining has deep roots in French Nouvelle Cuisine.

In creating this collection, we solicited input from chefs, restaurateurs, and writers: David Chang, Will Guidara, Daniel Humm, Corey Lee, Tatiana Levha, Pat Nourse, Enrique Olvera,

Daniel Patterson, Andrea Petrini, and René Redzepi. They provided insight into the dishes that were influential in their careers, and helped us right some glaring omissions. Not all of the chef-panelists are featured, but all have dishes that are currently making waves around the world: Olvera's mole madre; Humm's carrot tartare; Lee's thousand-year quail egg.

We expect (and hope) that this list will spark some debate among fine dining fanatics. For everyone else, here's a chance to bone up on your culinary history.

Canard à la presse
Frédéric Delair

Tour d'Argent
Paris, France
1890

Frédéric Delair didn't invent the duck press—that was likely the work of a Rouen man by the name of Méchenet earlier in the nineteenth century. What Delair created was a grand bit of tableside theater: he would place the carcass of a roasted duck—breasts removed—into an ornate silver press and crank the wheel, crushing the duck and draining its blood and juices into a silver bain-marie. He then cooked the duck juice down with Cognac and Madeira into a sauce to be poured over the sliced duck breast. Grandiose tableside plating was popular with chefs in Paris and the Lyon region through the 1960s, but nothing ever generated the same level of awe as canard à la presse.

Poularde en vessie
Fernand Point

La Pyramide
Vienne, France
1920s

In his book *Ma Gastronomie*, Fernand Point credits Marius Vettard of Café Neuf with inventing this dish, but it's Point who made it a symbol of Grande cuisine. Half a century before immersion circulators were invented for laboratory use, Point was sealing foie-gras-and-truffle-stuffed chickens in pig bladders and simmering them in a consommé of madeira and brandy, like a proto–sous vide. To the delight of his diners, Point would slice the ballooned bladder open tableside, revealing a perfectly cooked Bresse chicken within. From Bocuse to Boulud, chefs have been recreating *poularde en vessie* for nearly a century. Recently, Daniel Humm has revived in-bladder cooking at Eleven Madison Park in New York, with vegetables like celery root or asparagus in place of the chicken.

Red mullet with potato scales
Paul Bocuse

L'Auberge du Pont de Collonges
Lyon, France
1960s

The "scales" for Paul Bocuse's red mullet are made from slices of young potato brushed with egg yolk to form a single sturdy layer over the entire fillet. Bocuse himself was inspired by something he saw at a French food show—a dish of cold salmon topped with cucumber slices. Frédy Girardet would reimagine Bocuse's creation with red mullet and zucchini scales; Charlie Palmer made a version with scallops and potato chips; and Daniel Boulud and Gordon Ramsay would honor the original with more faithful recreations.

Saumon à l'oseille
Jean and Pierre Troisgros

La Maison Troisgros
Roanne, France
1962

Some chefs credit this dish with putting an end to the long-standing tradition of Western chefs overcooking fish. Every component is just-cooked, from the bright pink salmon (previously always sickly pale) to the bed of tart sorrel in a citrusy cream-and-white-wine sauce. The acidic flavors, lighter sauces, and restrained cooking times would become defining characteristics of nouvelle cuisine, a movement partially inspired by Japanese culinary culture. The combination of salmon and sorrel would also become a pillar of Lyonnais cuisine, recreated by French chefs for decades.

Bouillon de champignons comme un cappuccino
Alain Chapel

Restaurant Alain Chapel
Mionnay, France
1970s

Alain Chapel, who trained under Fernand Point, is one of the founding fathers of nouvelle cuisine. This soup course reimagines a cappuccino as an earthy, silky mushroom consommé topped with frothed broth. Crayfish tails hide under the foam in the soup, which is made without cream. Shades of Chapel's cappuccino can be seen in Eric Ripert's lobster cappuccino, Massimiliano Alajmo's cuttlefish capp, and Thomas Keller's version with forest mushrooms.

Pieds de cochon aux morilles
Pierre Koffmann

La Tante Claire
London, England
1977

Pierre Koffmann's pigs' trotters are a paragon of fine dining finesse and technique. The trotter has to be dehaired, skinned, and deboned with careful attention. From there, they're braised in a mixture of port, Madeira, brandy, and white wine, then stuffed with a farce of chicken breast, veal sweetbreads, and morels, and finally steamed and topped with a sauce resembling the cooking liquid. This dish is renowned for aggrandizing scrap cuts and rustic technique. When Marco Pierre White opened Harveys, it appeared on his menu as "Braised Pig's Trotter 'Pierre Koffmann.'"

Le gargouillou de
jeunes légumes
Michel Bras

Bras
Laguiole, France
1978

For each plate of *gargouillou,* the cooks at Bras artfully arrange petals, slices, shavings, fronds, and purées of fifty to sixty different vegetables—from foraged herbs and garden flowers to cucumbers and potatoes. Bras's seasonal and thoughtful approach to sourcing ingredients and presentation has echoed throughout fine dining in the decades since the dish's invention, reinforcing the importance of foraging and establishing a new plating aesthetic. The aftershocks of this dish are still shaking up menus today, inspiring dishes like David Kinch's Into the Vegetable Garden and Daniel Patterson's Abstraction of Garden in Early Winter.

Baked goat cheese
with garden lettuces
Alice Waters

Chez Panisse
Berkeley, California
1980

Alice Waters helped define California cuisine as a culinary movement that revolved around seasonal ingredients and responsible sourcing. This dish introduced many Americans to chèvre and exalted the pleasure of a simple garden salad. Soon, goat cheese and carefully prepared salads would appear on restaurant menus across the country. The salad became a symbol for California cuisine, and Waters's approach to cooking gave rise to farm-restaurants like Blue Hill at Stone Barns, run by Chez Panisse alum Dan Barber.

Riso, oro
e zafferano
Gualtiero Marchesi

Ristorante Gualtiero
Marchesi
Milan, Italy
1981

Stories of baroque-era food infused with gold inspired the Milanese tradition of serving risotto with raw egg yolks (and later saffron) so that it shone a pale yellow. Three centuries later, influenced by the artful plating of nouvelle cuisine, Gualtiero Marchesi introduced a new gold standard to Milanese risotto: he infused his risotto with enough saffron to turn it bright orange, then draped a square of edible gold leaf over the center. Marchesi would continue to bring dramatic plating to his dishes and, in so doing, forged a link between Italian fine dining and the visual arts.

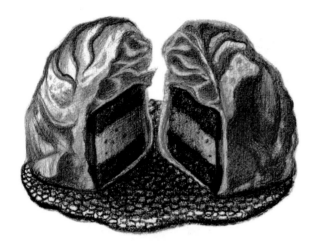

Feuilleté de truffe fraîche "bel humeur"
Bernard Pacaud

L'Ambroisie
Paris, France
Early 1980s

Bernard Pacaud is a Parisian chef whose cooking is deeply rooted in the Lyonnais culinary tradition. In the early 1980s, Pacaud made a canapé of "good mood" that transported diners back to Lyon in the 1960s. He baked layers of truffle and foie gras in a dome of puff pastry (Bocuse's *en croûte* style) and served it on a bed of puréed black truffles. The juxtaposition of crunchy and creamy textures with fatty-earthy flavors was a revelation. A few years later, Daniel Boulud served Sea Scallops "Black Tie" at Le Cirque: a reinterpretation of the *bel humeur* with thinner discs of black truffle and scallops in place of foie.

Chaud-froid d'oeuf au sirop d'érable
Alain Passard

Le Duc d'Enghien
Enghien-les-Bains, France
Early 1980s

The chefs of nouvelle cuisine introduced amuse-bouches—miniature dishes served before a meal—to excite the palate and prepare the diner for the meal to come. After leaving Le Duc d'Enghien to open his own restaurant in 1986, Passard continued serving the *chaud-froid d'oeuf* as part of a series of amuse-bouches that kick off the meal at Arpège. It's a dish of contrasts: warm poached egg yolk and cold sherry cream, sweet maple syrup and savory spices. The dish is served in an egg shell, a beautiful example of careful technique and delicate presentation. David Kinch cites Passard as a major influence and serves a version of the chaud-froid egg at his restaurant, Manresa.

Pizza with smoked salmon and caviar
Wolfgang Puck

Spago
Los Angeles, California
1982

Though some still refuse to recognize a distinct California style of pizza, Wolfgang Puck's influence on the pizza arts is undeniable. The "gourmet pizza"—topped with unexpected luxury ingredients—came to be in the 1980s when Puck began serving them at Spago in Beverly Hills. More important, the door to fine dining was thus opened to pizza and other everyday fare. For his part, Puck says that the smoked salmon and caviar pizza was an accident—he claims the kitchen was out of bread when a famous actress came into the restaurant asking for smoked salmon and brioche.

Purée de pommes de terre
Joël Robuchon

Jamin
Paris, France
1981

When Jamin was only three months old, Michelin inspectors awarded it one star for Joël Robuchon's stylized nouvelle cuisine—his masterful gelées and perfectly cubed vegetables—and his mashed potatoes. A few years later, Robuchon made a decisive turn toward more rustic cuisine influenced by his grandmother's recipes, but by then his *purée de pommes de terre* were already cemented in history. Robuchon's once outrageous two-to-one potato-to-butter ratio is now the standard for fine dining taters.

Flor de huevo y tartufo en grasa de oca con txistorra de dátiles
Juan Mari Arzak

Arzak
San Sebastián, Spain
1980s

Juan Mari Arzak brought the techniques of nouvelle cuisine (taught to him by Paul Bocuse) back to Spain, launching a culinary revolution that stripped back the richness in Basque cuisine and merged its rustic nature with refined techniques. In this iconic dish of New Basque cuisine, Arzak wrapped an egg tightly in plastic with truffle juice and duck fat before poaching it. The unwrapped egg emerged looking like a flower and was originally plated with chorizo-date mousse, mushrooms, and bread crumbs. The technique lives on, known simply as the "Arzak egg."

Foie gras en raviolis aux truffes dans un bouillon de poule
Alain Ducasse

Le Louis XV
Monte Carlo, Monaco
1987

Ducasse was one of the first French chefs to ignore the principles of nouvelle cuisine, reintroducing the richness of earlier decades. Ducasse rose to fame in Monte Carlo by combining the culinary traditions of Italy and his native Provence. Foie gras–stuffed ravioli is a Ducasse signature, rehashed by numerous French-inspired chefs, including Sottha Kuhn at Le Cirque and even Ducasse himself: in 2008 he served the foie ravioli in a sunchoke consommé at his New York restaurant Adour Alain Ducasse.

Black cod with miso
Nobu Matsuhisa

Matsuhisa
Los Angeles, California
1987

Nobu Matsuhisa introduced American diners to an idea of Japanese cuisine beyond teriyaki and sushi rolls with dishes like this one. Drawing on traditional curing techniques, Matsuhisa marinated black cod fillets in sake, miso, mirin, and sugar, then roasted the fish until the exterior was browned and crisp. Suddenly, miso wasn't just a soup, and once-cheap black cod rose in esteem and price all across Los Angeles and New York (where Matsuhisa opened his TriBeCa outpost Nobu).

Tagliatelle of oysters with caviar
Marco Pierre White

Harveys
London, England
1987

After training at La Tante Claire and Le Gavroche, Marco Pierre White opened Harveys in London and made a name for himself as England's brightest and fiercest young chef. Perhaps his most famous dish from this period was a set of five oyster shells, each filled with its oyster in a tangle of tagliatelle, beurre blanc, and a caviar garnish. White acknowledged the dish's French roots—oysters served in their shell with mousse (Le Gavroche), and langoustines prepared with tagliatelle (Belmond Le Manoir aux Quat'Saisons)—but it was his fresh perspective that modernized and legitimized London's culinary scene.

Sashimi of young maguro, mustard, soy-marinated egg-yolk sauce
Yoshihiro Murata

Kikunoi
Kyoto, Japan
1990s

While Yoshihiro Murata's cooking at Kikunoi shined a spotlight on Kyoto-style *kaiseki* cuisine in the 1990s, this dish became iconic for the liberties Murata took with traditional cooking. He was one of the first kaiseki chefs to popularize thick cuts of sashimi, and his soy-marinated egg-yolk sauce was a rich alternative to the typical simple, acidic accompaniments. Chefs like René Redzepi, Ferran Adrià, and Nobu Matsuhisa have credited Murata with emphasizing how aesthetics are integral to the dining experience and the importance of fermentation and umami.

Confit of ocean trout
Tetsuya Wakuda

Tetsuya's Restaurant
Sydney, Australia
1992

Tetsuya Wakuda synthesizes Japanese culinary philosophy, the French techniques he learned from chef Tony Bilson, and Sydney's local ingredients to create an ever-evolving seafood-focused menu. Wakuda's confit of ocean trout topped with kombu, fennel salad, and ocean-trout roe traces back to Pierre Koffmann's confit of salmon in goose fat. Wakuda's decision to use local ocean trout and olive oil and cook the fish at a low temperature to retain its color made him, and Sydney's fine dining scene, famous within the international dining community.

Oyster and Pearls
Thomas Keller

The French Laundry
Yountville, California
1994

This decadent dish—one of several staples on the French Laundry menu—is a playful interpretation of a natural phenomenon. The "pearls" in this case are tapioca balls—folded into a rich sabayon—and a fat quenelle of sevruga caviar. The oyster rests half-submerged in the sabayon, nestled next to the caviar. The French Laundry, hidden away in sleepy Yountville, forged new ground by merging rustic surroundings with ultra-luxury. Grant Achatz has called this dish (and his meal at the French Laundry) a turning point in his cooking career, noting that he'd never seen such a generous serving of caviar before, let alone as a garnish.

Whole baked abalone puff with diced chicken
Chan Yan Tak

Lung King Heen
Hong Kong, China
2000s

As the chef of the first Chinese restaurant to earn three Michelin stars, Chan Yan Tak is credited with introducing the world to fine dining Cantonese cuisine. Chan's whole abalone baked into puff pastry with diced chicken has become the stuff of legend for its expert preparation of abalone and its elevation of traditional dim-sum cookery.

Fine galette de champignons de Paris, foie gras marine au verjus, plantin
Pascal Barbot

Astrance
Paris, France
2005

Like the chefs before him who traveled to Japan and came back with nouvelle cuisine, Pascal Barbot pulled from culinary experiences in Australia, Indonesia, and Mexico to forge a new path for French cuisine. His focus on vegetables and products in their natural state was revolutionary at the time. For his iconic foie-gras-and-mushroom galette, he layered products rarely served raw in France—thinly sliced Paris mushrooms and *verjus*-marinated foie gras—into a towering mille-feuille-like wedge, served with hazelnut oil and lemon curd.

Spherical olives
Ferran Adrià

El Bulli
Roses, Spain
2005

While other chefs were focused on showcasing ingredients in their natural state, Ferran Adrià was building a mythic temple of modernist cuisine in Spain. Adrià's stated goal with many of his impossible-seeming creations was to create a better version of an ingredient than nature could offer. To make these spherical olives, he puréed green olives and dropped spoonfuls of the strained juice into a liquid alginate solution, which reacts with the calcium in the olive to form a gel-like sphere. After marinating overnight, the "olives" are served with a gin-and-vermouth spray to create the effect of a dirty martini.

Hot Potato, Cold Potato
Grant Achatz

Alinea
Chicago, Illinois
2005

Achatz's exuberant avant-garde cooking has kept Chicago firmly in the fine dining conversation for more than a decade. The hot potato in this classic dish from Alinea is a sphere of Yukon Gold that has been cooked in clarified butter, then skewered with a piece of chive and cubes of parmesan and butter. It rests in mid-air, crowned with a slice of truffle, over a creamy soup of potato and truffle. The two potatoes come together theatrically when the diner pulls out the pin and the skewered ingredients fall into the cold soup below.

Eggs Benedict
Wylie Dufresne

wd~50
New York City, New York
2005

Part of a relentlessly imaginative line of chefs that includes Heston Blumenthal and Ferran Adrià, Wylie Dufresne took beloved and well-known American foods and completely reinvented them at his New York restaurant wd~50. This dish is a sum of many parts: deep-fried cubes of hollandaise (stabilized with hydrocolloids and coated in Thomas' English-muffin crumbs); fudgy-textured egg yolks cooked sous vide; and vellum-thin slices of Canadian bacon. The dish simultaneously surprises diners with its textural remixes and rings familiar with its flavors.

Edible Stones
Andoni Luis Aduriz

Mugaritz
San Sebastián, Spain
2005

Before your meal at Mugaritz, two envelopes are placed in front of you; one reads 150 MINUTES … SUBMIT! and the other 150 MINUTES … REBEL! Whichever card you choose, the meal will unfold the same way, but Andoni Luis Aduriz believes that much of our dining enjoyment comes down to perception. This dish is the perfect example: in front of you is a bowl of stones, two edible and the rest actual stones from the nearby river. The edible stones are boiled potatoes coated in a paste made from *agalita* (an edible white clay), lactose, salt, and water that sets into a rigid gray coating. The difference between a jarring find and a soft and creamy potato comes down to choice.

Sound of the Sea
Heston Blumenthal

The Fat Duck
Bray, England
2007

Blumenthal's cerebral but lighthearted approach and trompe l'oeil creations earned him three Michelin stars at the Fat Duck and celebrity status around the world. The Sound of the Sea is possibly the most dramatic example of his brand of cuisine: a fragrant miniature beachscape of tapioca sand, sea foam, and pieces of fish and pickled seaweed, accompanied by an iPod hidden in a conch shell. The diner pulls headphones from the shell and listens to the calls of seagulls and waves crashing on a beach while eating the sea-centric dish, transporting them to the seaside and theoretically intensifying the briny flavors.

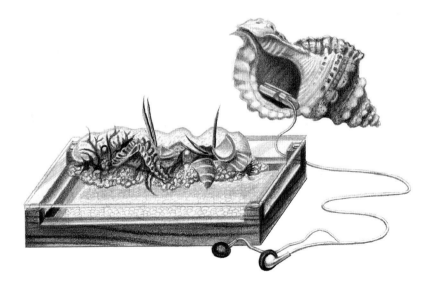

Pickled Vegetables
René Redzepi

Noma
Copenhagen, Denmark
2007

New Nordic cuisine took the world by storm a decade ago and virtually eclipsed all other fine dining for a few years, largely thanks to René Redzepi and his restaurant, Noma. The dish that first sparked the nonstop chatter was this assembly of colorful pickled vegetables shaved thin, curled into rings, and arranged with flowers and herbs on a plate coated with bone marrow. Redzepi made vegetables, foraging, and fermentation part of the modern vanguard and opened the door for other Nordic chefs to reimagine their regional cuisine.

Beet Rose
Daniel Patterson

Coi
San Francisco, California
2011

Daniel Patterson's beet rose represents an evolution of California cuisine: produce is still the prominent feature, but simple preparations are spurned in favor of precise technique and painstaking plating. Each beet "petal" is sliced from the core of a roasted beet, dipped in beet juice, and delicately added to the flower until a full rose is formed. The rose is then transferred onto a base of beet purée, aerated yogurt, and rose-petal ice. Earlier this year, René Redzepi crafted an homage to the beet rose using rhubarb cooked in rose oil and kelp.

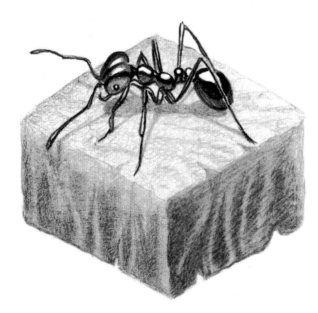

Ants and Pineapple
Alex Atala

D.O.M.
São Paulo, Brazil
2000s

Alex Atala and his Brazilian restaurant, D.O.M., were among the first to push South America into the fine dining limelight. Atala is a champion of Amazonian ingredients and the importance of supporting indigenous communities. In the rain forest of Amazonas, Atala discovered the intense flavor of lemongrass and ginger given off by ants. At D.O.M., he served an intact dried ant on a cube of fresh pineapple, effectively destigmatizing bugs as ingredients in fine dining kitchens. Ants and other insects have begun to show up on menus around the world ever since. **LP**

Premium Caribbean Rums crafted with Natural ingredients

Beyond the White Tablecloth

BY LUCAS TURNER

ILLUSTRATIONS BY JOHN LISLE

In the Western world, our notion of "fine dining" tends to be pretty francocentric. Fair enough. For much of the twentieth century, it's been possible to draw a straight line from most high-end restaurants back to Paris, Lyon, Roanne, or Laguiole. But other refined dining traditions have existed throughout history and across the globe.

The closest in spirit are the royal court cuisines of Asia. Like French haute cuisine, these traditions are highly elaborate, prepared by specialized, professional cooks who prize quality and exclusivity in terms of the season's choicest pickings (or, more often, imported or out-of-season delicacies). Like the monarchies they catered to, many of these traditions are now the stuff of history, but a few have persevered.

Chinese Imperial Cuisine

The high cuisine of China's Imperial Era (from the Qin Dynasty, 221 BCE, to the Qing, 1911 CE) is most often associated with Beijing, China's more or less continuous capital since the fifteenth century.

Dining in the Forbidden City, Beijing's imperial palace, was grandiose and elaborate and as much about quantity as quality. The Dowager Empress Cixi (1835–1908) legendarily demanded no fewer than one hundred dishes at her meals, and snacks could be beckoned for at any moment. A typical meal for China's last emperor, Pu Yi (1906–1967), consisted of thirty dishes. According to his autobiography, the dishes prepared from the main imperial kitchens were often made well in advance, wilting, sagging, and growing cold throughout the day; the vast majority of the food was ultimately destined for the trash (or the palace's fleet of resourceful eunuchs).

TYPICAL DISHES: Shark's fins, bird's nests, and bear's paws were fixtures at the imperial table, along with stir-fried mutton, wine-preserved duck, goose fat and sugar dumplings, and myriad hot soups, congees, and confections. Ice was kept frozen in engineered caves. Peking duck is considered by many to be a Forbidden City invention—ex-palace chefs helped open Quanjude (now an international chain) in 1864, using a palace technique for roasting ducks over a fruitwood fire.

TODAY: The kitchens of lower court members also played a role in developing and evolving imperial cookery. Some developed into iconic styles of their own, such as Tan family cuisine (*tan jia cai*), named after the nineteenth-century court member Tan Zongjun, and Man-Han banquet style, named after an infamous three-day banquet that blended the robust and rich dishes of the northeastern Manchu with the more delicate cuisine of the Han. Today, Tan family cuisine restaurant Guo Yao Xiao Ju in Beijing serves dishes like creamy, gelatinous *nongtang yudu* (fish stomach soup), thousand-year yak's ear (crispy ear cartilage set in gelatin), fried crepes stuffed with smoked duck and chives, and tender bamboo shoots in chili oil. Beijing's Fangshan restaurant, opened by former imperial chefs after the closing of the Forbidden City in 1924, specializes in Man-Han banquet cuisine, bird's nest soup, sesame flatbreads stuffed with minced pork, and braised camel foot.

Thai Royal Court Cuisine

The Chakri Dynasty began ruling Thailand in 1782, but its last absolute monarchy effectively ended in 1932, when the Khana Ratsadon, a small faction of military officers and civilians, overthrew the royal family. But continuing into the 1960s, the Grand Palace in Bangkok served as a finishing school for the upper class, where daughters were sent to learn all aspects of domesticity, including cooking and vegetable and fruit carving. Malcolm Smith, Queen Saovabha's (1864–1919) physician, remarked in his journal that the Grand Palace "was a town of women, controlled by women." Unlike many other fine dining traditions, women, not men, were historically the ones cooking for the royal court.

TYPICAL DISHES: Daytime meals at the Grand Palace tended to be light, to account for the often sweltering heat. Come evening, small appetizers would begin to trickle out from the kitchens: crisp coconut cakes garnished with minced meat and curry paste; green rice topped with dried, sweetened fish; flower-scented rice with salted shrimp. Cucumbers were carved to look like mango leaves and eggplants sliced into flowers. For dinner, rice from the emperor's private paddies was served alongside hearty side dishes like red beef curry with fried clams, or curry with green peppercorns and fried squid.

Desserts included jasmine-scented duck with egg-yolk threads, and fruit in coconut fat and iced syrup. Royal cuisine reached its apex during ceremonies. For one Thai New Year celebration at the palace in the early twentieth century, rose petals were candied and reassembled as flowers, and poultry "strings" were made by meticulously peeling sugar-braised chicken and caramelizing the strands.

TODAY: As the Thai monarchy has diminished, its cuisine has become less and less distinguishable from that of everyday Thai. Thai chef M. L. Sirichalerm Svasti (aka Chef McDang), who grew up eating at the palace with his great-aunt Queen Rambhai Barni (1904–1984), says that the food differed mostly in its presentation. Made in the palace style, a common *nam prik pla tu* (whole fried mackerel with chili sauce) would be fried, meticulously deboned, have its flesh reattached, then be fried again to maintain its whole appearance.

According to chef and Thai food historian David Thompson, Thai royal cuisine is "extinct," surviving mainly through cookbooks and journals of the period. However, Thompson's Nahm restaurants—first in London and later in Bangkok—have been greatly influenced by royal Thai cuisine. Thompson was mentored by the late Khun Sombat Janphetchara, daughter of a Grand Palace chef and "heir to a tradition of great culinary refinement." At Nahm, Thompson draws from his collection of five hundred cookbooks to inspire his dishes, like smoked fish and peanut dumplings and *geng dtay plaa* (fish stomach stew with jackfruit).

Kaiseki

In Japanese, *kaiseki* has two different spellings and meanings. The first, most common spelling translates roughly to "pocket stone," a reference to the warm stone that monks in training traditionally slipped into their robes to quell their hunger pangs. This spelling of kaiseki alludes to the austere tea ceremony tradition (*chanoyu*) historically practiced by Zen monasteries beginning in the twelfth century, when the Japanese priest Eisai brought green tea seeds and the tea ceremony practices he learned at Chinese monasteries back to Japan. Tea master Sen Rikyu (1522–1591) is credited with popularizing *cha-kaiseki*, the pre-tea ceremony meal of soup and three side dishes.

The second, older spelling of kaiseki translates roughly to "seated gathering," and is used to describe the luxurious, multi-course eating styles of the daimyo—regional lords who ruled feudal Japan from the fourteenth to the late nineteenth century.

TYPICAL DISHES: The elaborate, sometimes days-long meals of the daimyo might have consisted of dishes like fermented crucian carp sushi, meats like crane and sea cucumber entrails, and delicate soups of rapeseed flowers and tiny fish. Some daimyo insisted on their own house-made tableware that, like the food, changed with the seasons: brighter colors and flatter surfaces for the summer, muted, curved bowls for the winter.

TODAY: Though the two kaiseki traditions have influenced each other, modern kaiseki restaurants take their cue from the more luxurious daimyo version. At third-generation kaiseki chef Yoshihiro Murata's Kikunoi restaurant in Kyoto, the restaurant's artwork and furniture shift to coincide with each new season. A typical spring meal at Kikunoi might begin with a *sakizuke* (small bite) of sake-steamed sea bream milt, followed by an assortment of small plates (*hassun*) that set the seasonal tone of the meal: steamed lily petals with salmon roe, broiled squid assembled into a fern, dashi-simmered yams shaped like butterflies. The courses build on one another, becoming more robust. *Kinome* and pink sea bream sushi precedes the grilled *yakimono* course: cherry salmon grilled over cherry wood. The meal finishes with a hot pot of wakame seaweed and just-harvested bamboo shoots. Delicacy and seasonality continue to be featured in desserts like mugwort rice cakes with red bean paste and almond jelly dotted with gelatinous Thai basil seeds. According to the restaurant, service is "visible yet unobtrusive." Some scholars maintain that Japan's strong sense of hospitality, *omotenashi*, evolved out of the kaiseki tea ceremony tradition, in which the host takes care of the guests without the expectation of reciprocity.

Korean Royal Cuisine

During the Choson Dynasty (1392–1910) the royal court of Seoul ate a cuisine that brought together regional delicacies from around the country for the enjoyment of the royal family. Palace food was cooked almost exclusively by women, generally from lower-class families, who worked their way up through a seven-to-ten-year apprenticeship under the elder palace cooks. Apprenticeships generally started at the age of twelve and ended with a coming-of-age ceremony in which the women received an official rank and position. Unless given permission to marry by the king, women would spend the rest of their lives in the palace kitchens. Dishes for the king and queen were always brought to three separate tables by attending palace women (*sura sanggung*). The royal court believed that silver would change color if it touched poisoned food, so silver tableware was often used and the sura sanggung diligently checked every dish for poisoning before it was served.

TYPICAL DISHES: Much of the food consisted of traditional dishes, only with higher quality ingredients and an abundance of garnishes. Breakfast and dinner were the main meals, called sura, served to the palace royals each day. They generally included two rice dishes, two different soups, three kimchis, two different stews, three sauces, one steamed dish, and twelve side dishes. Soups like *naengmyeon*, a cold buckwheat noodle soup in a beef broth, or *yeolguja tang*, a hot pot–style soup of thinly sliced vegetables and meat arranged in a colorful pattern, were the largest dishes of the meal. Side dishes (*banchan*) included seasoned vegetables like daikon and deodeok root, small plates of meat like *chotkal* (fermented fish innards or flesh), and *chorigae* (boiled meat or vegetables in a soy-based sauce).

TODAY: Royal cuisine is still practiced at Jihwaja, a restaurant founded in 1991 by Hwang Hye-sung, a government-certified royal cuisine master who learned under the late Han Hui-sun, a lead cook in the royal kitchen of the Choson Dynasty's final two emperors. Jihwaja serves an assortment of elaborate set menus ranging in size and price. The deluxe royal degustation menu, *gungjung manchan*, features sixteen courses of dishes like beef skewers with fresh ginseng and bellflower root, pomegranate dumpling soup, and treats like a creamy milk porridge and *gaesong yakgwa*, a fried, multilayered pastry of sesame oil and honey. Everything is lightly seasoned in comparison to the spicy, salty Korean dishes we generally imagine. "The flavors of [court cuisine] are not too strong; they highlight the original flavors of the ingredients themselves," says Lee Soon-hwa, Jihwaja's food and beverage director.

Mughlai Cuisine

Mughlai cooking is that of the royal court of the Mughal Empire, which ruled over a majority of the Indian subcontinent from the early sixteenth century until it was toppled by British colonialism in the nineteenth. The empire was founded by warrior prince/foodie Babur the Tiger (1483–1530), of Turkic-Mongol descent. The high cuisine of his empire was an amalgamation of Persian, Islamic, and Turkic-Mongolian aesthetics and foodways. In his journals, Babur remarks that "Hindustan is a country of few charms," lacking "grapes, musk melons, first-rate fruit, no ice or cold water, no good bread or cooked food in the bazaars," which he dutifully introduced to his newly conquered territories as soon as he took power.

With the reign of Akbar (1542–1605), the third Mughal emperor, food was raised to the level of state concern: ice was being rushed from the Himalayas, ghee (clarified butter) became the empire's fat of choice, and melons, stone fruit, and nuts were grown in profusion. Akbar traveled through his territories alongside roving kitchen tents staffed with a small army of cooks.

TYPICAL DISHES: Like those of Imperial Beijing, royal meals were often spontaneous and consisted of no fewer than one hundred dishes, organized into three classes: *safiyana* (fasting food), meatless, grain-based dishes like dry rice and lentils; meat-and-grain dishes like spiced *biryanis* of rice and chicken with fruits and nuts; and meat and vegetables cooked in ghee. Mountains of fresh fruit and confections accompanied the savory dishes on ornate, jeweled dishware. Everything was extravagantly plated: one version of rice pilau made for Emperor Akbar called for each grain to be painted red and white to resemble pomegranate seeds; another, mounded to house small birds that would fly out when opened.

Omnivorous in appetite, the Mughals readily adopted the customs and cuisines of the conquered. "Mughlai cuisine brought together the cookery of central Asia, Persia, and Hindustan by combining different dishes from each of these traditions in one meal," writes Dr. Elizabeth Collingham in her book *Curry: A Tale of Cooks and Conquerors*. The imperial kitchen, Collingham explains, featured both Hindu and Persian traditions: "Thin chapattis of Hindu provenance as well as the thick wheat breads, stuffed with honey, sugar, and almonds, loved by the Persians. Persian cooks prepared sugar-coated almonds, pastries, and quince jams, while Indian cooks made pickles and chutneys, sweet limes, curds, and green vegetables."

TODAY: With the passing of the monarchy, Mughlai cooking mostly lives on in northern Indian cooking. Modern versions of Mughlai cuisine can be found at restaurants like Karim's in Old Delhi, the walled city at the center of New Delhi that served as the Mughal Empire's capital until the nineteenth century. Founded in 1913 by Haji Karimuddin, son of a royal cook in the kitchen of the final Mughal Emperor, Bahadur Shah II (1775–1862), Karim's specializes in classic Mughlai fare, like green chili and mutton kebabs, and *badam pasanda* curry with almonds and lamb—albeit in a much more humble environment than the historic Mughal courts. **LP**

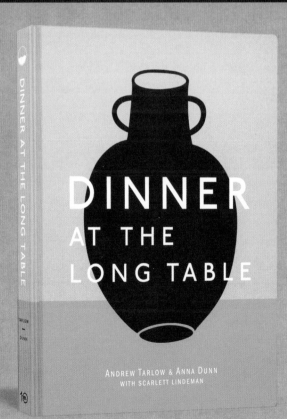

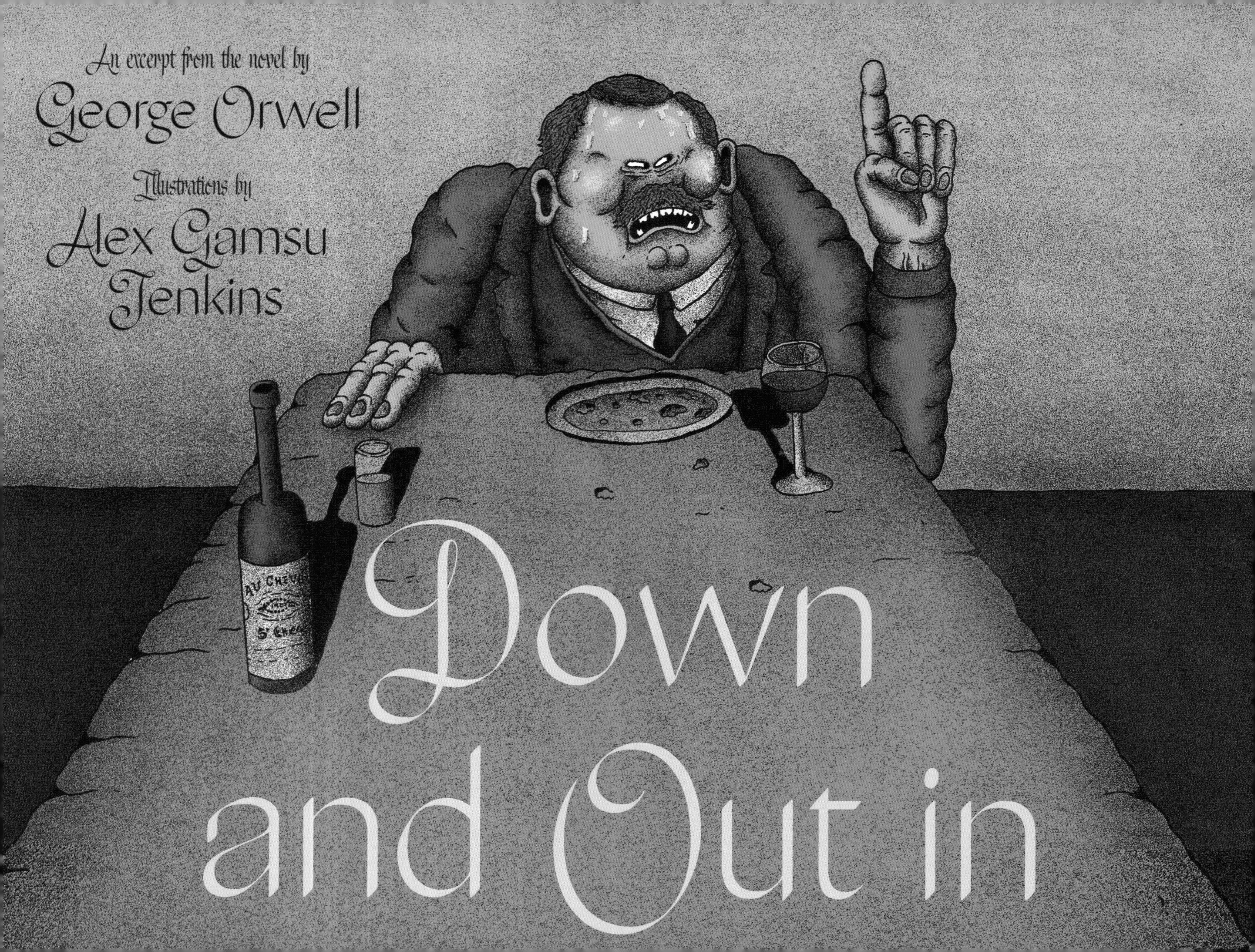

Down and Out in

An excerpt from the novel by

George Orwell

Illustrations by

Alex Gamsu Jenkins

Paris and London

uck *Kitchen Confidential.*

Not really, but fuck it anyway.

George Orwell was there long, long before me, "ripping the lid off" fine dining and depicting, in unsparing terms, the filth, the language, the subculture, the complete disconnect between what was seen in the dining room and what happened behind the kitchen doors. Published in 1933, *Down and Out in Paris and London* is based on young Eric Blair's experiences at the grand "Hôtel X" in Paris, where he worked as a dishwasher after returning from a deeply transformative and embittering experience as a colonial policeman in Burma.

Orwell's kitchen world remains immediately recognizable to anyone who has spent time working in a busy restaurant: the characters, the alternate realities of the front of house and back of house, the cruelty, the pressure, the odd, insular camaraderie and injured pride unique to cooks and perhaps circus folk. Orwell painted, for the first time, a portrait of a world few outsiders had seen—or wanted to see—and, long before I did it with *Kitchen Confidential,* he pissed off a lot of restaurateurs who would rather have kept it all quiet.

The book, whose original working title was *A Scullion's Diary,* and then, briefly, *The Confessions of a Dishwasher,* was Eric Blair's first; it was also the first time he used the name Orwell. It has been suggested he used the pseudonym to separate his middle-class family from any disgrace resulting from either the events described in the book or the very fact of its writing.

Down and Out in Paris and London changed my life. It was the direct inspiration for *Kitchen Confidential,* the text I had in mind with every page. I read it as a young dishwasher in Provincetown, Massachusetts. I was seventeen and in the first year of what would become nearly thirty years in the business. It was still the good old, bad old days of professional cooking, when kitchen brigades truly were the last refuge of the misfit and the fuckup. I was the newest, worst member of the kitchen crew, a regular target of dirty pots and pans thrown in my general direction. I was surrounded by what seemed, at least to my untrained eyes, like madmen and drunks who still somehow managed to pump out astonishing quantities

of food with what looked very much like competence. To them, I was not yet even worthy of a name, as it was unlikely that I'd last. I was called Mel, or "the Mel" when referred to in the third person; it was short for *mal carne* ("bad meat," in Italian). I limped home every night, exhausted, reeking, filthy, and depressed. I wanted their love. I wanted the kind of respect the veteran cooks had for each other. I wanted to be called by my name.

During those times, *Down and Out in Paris and London* sustained me. It made me feel I was not alone, that I was part of something, a tradition, a cult, a secret... something... that stretched back to the 1920s in Paris, and beyond. It held me together, gave me the strength to show up again the next day and the next, until they did give me my name back and I went home having won, for the first time in my life, a modicum of respect from other human beings whose respect I wanted. I went home respecting myself—another first.

It's the story of a middle-class boy who found himself in, or rather put himself into, the rough world of hard physical labor. It inspired me to keep on. It made me want to be a cook. And I owe everything to that.

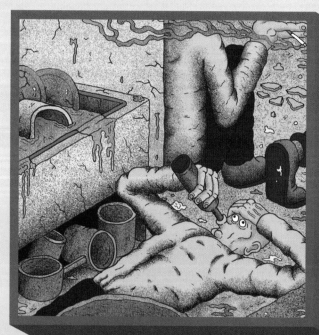

By far my best time at the hotel was when I went to help the waiter on the fourth floor. We worked in a small pantry, which communicated with the *cafeterie* by service lifts. It was delightfully cool after the cellars, and the work was chiefly polishing silver and glasses, which is a humane job.

Valenti, the waiter, was a decent sort, and treated me almost as an equal when we were alone, though he had to speak roughly when there was anyone else present, for it does not do for a waiter to be friendly with *plongeurs*. He used sometimes to tip me five francs when he had had a good day. He was a comely youth, aged twenty-four but looking eighteen, and, like most waiters, he carried himself well and knew how to wear his clothes. With his black tailcoat and white tie, fresh face and sleek brown hair, he looked just like an Eton boy; yet he had earned his living since he was twelve, and worked his way up literally from the gutter. Crossing the Italian frontier without a passport, and selling chestnuts from a barrow on the northern boulevards, and being given fifty days' imprisonment in London for working without a permit, and being made love to by a rich old woman in a hotel, who gave him a diamond ring and afterwards accused him of stealing it, were among his experiences. I used to enjoy talking to him, at slack times when we sat smoking down the lift shaft.

My bad day was when I washed up for the dining room. I had not to wash the plates, which were done in the kitchen, but only the other crockery, silver, knives and glasses; yet, even so, it meant thirteen hours' work, and I used between thirty and forty dishcloths during the day. The antiquated methods used in France double the work of washing up. Plate-racks are unheard-of, and there are no soap-flakes, only the treacly soft soap, which refuses to lather in the hard Paris water. I worked in a dirty, crowded little den, a pantry and scullery combined, which gave straight on the dining room. Besides washing up, I had to fetch the waiters' food and serve them at table; most of them were intolerably insolent, and I had to use my fists more than once to get common civility. The person who normally washed up was a woman, and they made her life a misery.

It was amusing to look round the filthy little scullery and think that only a double door was between us

and the dining room. There sat the customers in all their splendour—spotless tablecloths, bowls of flowers, mirrors and gilt cornices and painted cherubim; and here, just a few feet away, we in our disgusting filth. For it really was disgusting filth. There was no time to sweep the floor till evening, and we slithered about in a compound of soapy water, lettuce leaves, torn paper, and trampled food. A dozen waiters with their coats off, showing their sweaty armpits, sat at the table mixing salads and sticking their thumbs into the cream pots. The room had a dirty, mixed smell of food and sweat. Everywhere in the cupboards, behind the piles of crockery, were squalid stores of food that the waiters had stolen. There were only two sinks, and no washing basin, and it was nothing unusual for a waiter to wash his face in the water in which clean crockery was rinsing. But the customers saw nothing of this. There were a coconut mat and a mirror outside the dining room door, and the waiters used to preen themselves up and go in looking the picture of cleanliness.

It is an instructive sight to see a waiter going into a hotel dining room. As he passes the door a sudden change comes over him. The set of his shoulders alters; all the dirt and hurry and irritation have dropped off in an instant. He glides over the carpet, with a solemn priest-like air. I remember our assistant maître d'hôtel, a fiery Italian, pausing at the dining room door to address an apprentice who had broken a bottle of wine. Shaking his fist above his head he yelled (luckily the door was more or less soundproof):

'*Tu me fais*—Do you call yourself a waiter, you young bastard? You a waiter! You're not fit to scrub floors in the brothel your mother came from. *Maquereau!*'

Words failing him, he turned to the door; and as he opened it he delivered a final insult in the same manner as Squire Western in *Tom Jones*.

Then he entered the dining room and sailed across it dish in hand, graceful as a swan. Ten seconds later he was bowing reverently to a customer. And you could not help thinking, as you saw him bow and smile, with that benign smile of the trained waiter, that the customer was put to shame by having such an aristocrat to serve him.

This washing up was a thoroughly odious job—not hard, but boring and silly beyond words. It is dreadful to think that some people spend their whole decades at such occupations. The woman whom I replaced was quite sixty years old, and she stood at the sink thirteen hours a day, six days a week, the year round; she was, in addition, horribly bullied by the waiters. She gave out that she had once been an actress—actually, I imagine, a prostitute; most prostitutes end as charwomen. It was strange to see that in spite of her age and her life she still wore a bright blonde wig, and darkened her eyes and painted her face like a girl of twenty. So apparently even a seventy-eight-hour week can leave one with some vitality.

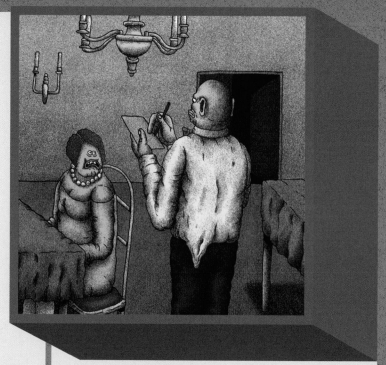

On my third day at the hotel the chef du personnel, who had generally spoken to me in quite a pleasant tone, called me up and said sharply:

'Here, you, shave that moustache off at once! *Nom de Dieu,* who ever heard of a *plongeur* with a moustache?'

I began to protest, but he cut me short. 'A *plongeur* with a moustache—nonsense! Take care I don't see you with it tomorrow.'

On the way home I asked Boris what this meant. He shrugged his shoulders. 'You must do what he says, *mon ami.* No one in the hotel wears a moustache, except the cooks. I should have thought you would have noticed it. Reason? There is no reason. It is the custom.'

I saw that it was an etiquette, like not wearing a white tie with a dinner jacket, and shaved off my moustache. Afterwards I found out the explanation of the custom, which is this: waiters in good hotels do not wear moustaches, and to show their superiority they decree that *plongeurs* shall not wear them either; and the cooks wear their moustaches to show their contempt for the waiters.

This gives some idea of the elaborate caste system existing in a hotel. Our staff, amounting to about a hundred and ten, had their prestige graded as accurately as that of soldiers, and a cook or waiter was as much above a *plongeur* as a captain above a private. Highest of all came the manager, who could sack anybody, even the cooks. We never saw the *patron,* and all we knew of him was that his meals had to be prepared more carefully than that of the customers; all the discipline of the hotel depended on the manager. He was a conscientious man,

and always on the lookout for slackness, but we were too clever for him. A system of service bells ran through the hotel, and the whole staff used these for signalling to one another. A long ring and a short ring, followed by two more long rings, meant that the manager was coming, and when we heard it we took care to look busy.

Below the manager came the maître d'hôtel. He did not serve at table, unless to a lord or someone of that kind, but directed the other waiters and helped with the catering. His tips, and his bonus from the champagne companies (it was two francs for each cork he returned to them), came to two hundred francs a day. He was in a position quite apart from the rest of the staff, and took his meals in a private room, with silver on the table and two apprentices in clean white jackets to serve him. A little below the head waiter came the head cook, drawing about five thousand francs a month; he dined in the kitchen, but at a separate table, and one of the apprentice cooks waited on him. Then came the *chef du personnel*; he drew only fifteen hundred francs a month, but he wore a black coat and did no manual work, and he could sack *plongeurs* and fine waiters. Then came the other cooks, drawing anything between three thousand and seven hundred and fifty francs a month; then the waiters, making about seventy francs a day in tips, besides a small retaining fee; then the laundresses and sewing women; then the apprentice waiters, who received no tips, but were paid seven hundred and fifty francs a month; then the *plongeurs,* also at seven hundred and fifty francs; then the chambermaids, at five or six hundred francs a month; and lastly the *cafetiers*, at five hundred a month. We of the *cafeterie* were the very dregs of the hotel, despised and *tutoied* by everyone.

There were various others—the office employees, called generally couriers, the storekeeper, the cellarman, some porters and pages, the ice man, the bakers, the night watchman, the doorkeeper. Different jobs were done by different races. The office employees and the cooks and sewing women were French, the waiters Italians and Germans (there is hardly such a thing as a French waiter in Paris), the *plongeurs* of every race in Europe, beside Arabs and Negroes. French was the lingua franca, even the Italians speaking it to one another.

All the departments had their special perquisites. In all Paris hotels it is the custom to sell the broken bread to bakers for eight sous a pound, and the kitchen scraps to pig keepers for a trifle, and to divide the proceeds of this among the *plongeurs*. There was much pilfering, too. The waiters all stole food—in fact, I seldom saw a waiter trouble to eat the rations provided for him by the hotel—and the cooks did it on a larger scale in the kitchen, and we in the *cafeterie* swilled illicit tea and coffee. The cellarman stole brandy. By a rule of the hotel the waiters were not allowed to keep stores of spirits, but had to go to the cellarman for each drink as it was ordered. As the cellarman poured out the drinks he would set aside perhaps a teaspoonful from each glass, and he amassed quantities in this way. He

would sell you the stolen brandy for five sous a swig if he thought he could trust you.

There were thieves among the staff, and if you left money in your coat pockets it was generally taken. The doorkeeper, who paid our wages and searched us for stolen food, was the greatest thief in the hotel. Out of my five hundred francs a month, this man actually managed to cheat me of a hundred and fourteen francs in six weeks. I had asked to be paid daily, so the doorkeeper paid me sixteen francs each evening, and, by not paying for Sundays (for which of course payment was due), pocketed sixty-four francs. Also, I sometimes worked on a Sunday, for which, though I did not know it, I was entitled to an extra twenty-five francs. The doorkeeper never paid me this either, and so made away with another seventy-five francs. I only realized during my last week that I was being cheated, and, as I could prove nothing, only twenty-five francs were refunded. The doorkeeper played similar tricks on any employee who was fool enough to be taken in. He called himself a Greek, but in reality he was an Armenian. After knowing him I saw the force of the proverb 'Trust a snake before a Jew and a Jew before a Greek, but don't trust an Armenian.'

There were queer characters among the waiters. One was a gentleman—a youth who had been educated at a university, and had had a well-paid job in a business office. He had caught a venereal disease, lost his job, drifted, and now considered himself lucky to be a waiter. Many of the waiters had slipped into France without passports, and one or two of them were spies—it is a

common profession for a spy to adopt. One day there was a fearful row in the waiters' dining room between Morandi, a dangerous-looking man with eyes set too far apart, and another Italian. It appeared that Morandi had taken the other man's mistress. The other man, a weakling and obviously frightened of Morandi, was threatening vaguely.

Morandi jeered at him. 'Well, what are you going to do about it? I've slept with your girl, slept with her three times. It was fine. What can you do, eh?'

'I can denounce you to the secret police. You are an Italian spy.'

Morandi did not deny it. He simply produced a razor from his tail pocket and made two swift strokes in the air, as though slashing a man's cheeks open. Whereat the other waiter took it back.

The queerest type I ever saw in the hotel was an 'extra.' He had been engaged at twenty-five francs for the day to replace the Magyar, who was ill. He was a Serbian, a thick set nimble fellow of about twenty-five, speaking six languages, including English. He seemed to know all about hotel work, and up till midday he worked like a slave. Then, as soon as it had struck twelve, he turned sulky, shirked his work, stole wine, and finally crowned all by loafing about openly with a pipe in his mouth. Smoking, of course, was forbidden under severe penalties. The manager himself heard of it and came down to interview the Serbian, fuming with rage.

'What the devil do you mean by smoking here?' he cried.

'What the devil do you mean by having a face like that?' answered the Serbian, calmly.

I cannot convey the blasphemy of such a remark. The head cook, if a *plongeur* had spoken to him like that, would have thrown a saucepan of hot soup in his face. The manager said instantly, 'You're sacked!' and at two o'clock the Serbian was given his twenty-five francs and duly sacked. Before he went out Boris asked him in Russian what game he was playing. He said the Serbian answered:

'Look here, *mon vieux*, they've got to pay me a day's wages if I work up to midday, haven't they? That's the law. And where's the sense of working after I get my wages? So I'll tell you what I do. I go to a hotel and get a job as an extra, and up to midday I work hard. Then, the moment it's struck twelve, I start raising such hell that they've no choice but to sack me. Neat, eh? Most days I'm sacked by half past twelve; today it was two o'clock; but I don't care, I've saved four hours' work. The only trouble is, one can't do it at the same hotel twice.'

It appeared that he had played this game at half the hotels and restaurants in Paris. It is probably quite an easy game to play during the summer, though the hotels protect themselves against it as well as they can by means of a black list.

In a few days I had grasped the main principles on which

the hotel was run. The thing that would astonish anyone coming for the first time into the service quarters of a hotel would be the fearful noise and disorder during the rush hours. It is something so different from the steady work in a shop or a factory that it looks at first sight like mere bad management. But it is really quite unavoidable, and for this reason. Hotel work is not particularly hard, but by its nature it comes in rushes and cannot be economized. You cannot, for instance, grill a steak two hours before it is wanted; you have to wait till the last moment, by which time a mass of other work has accumulated, and then do it all together, in frantic haste. The result is that at mealtimes everyone is doing two men's work, which is impossible without noise and quarrelling. Indeed the quarrels are a necessary part of the process, for the pace would never be kept up if everyone did not accuse everyone else of idling. It was for this reason that during the rush hours the whole staff raged and cursed like demons. At those times there was scarcely a verb in the hotel except *foutre*. A girl in the bakery, aged sixteen, used oaths that would have defeated a cabman. (Did not Hamlet say, 'cursing like a scullion'? No doubt Shakespeare had watched scullions at work.) But we are not losing our heads and wasting time; we were just stimulating one another for the effort of packing four hours' work into two hours.

What keeps a hotel going is the fact that the employees take a genuine pride in their work, beastly and silly though it is. If a man idles, the others soon find him out, and conspire against him to get him sacked. Cooks, waiters, and *plongeurs* differ greatly in outlook, but they are all alike in being proud of their efficiency.

Undoubtedly the most workmanlike class, and the least servile, are the cooks. They do not earn quite so much as waiters, but their prestige is higher and their employment steadier.

The cook does not look upon himself as a servant, but as a skilled workman; he is generally called 'un ouvrier' which a waiter never is. He knows his power—knows that he alone makes or mars a restaurant, and that if he is five minutes late everything is out of gear. He despises the whole non-cooking staff, and makes it a point of honour to insult everyone below the head waiter. And he takes a genuine artistic pride in his work, which demands very great skill. It is not the cooking that is so difficult, but the doing everything to time. Between breakfast and luncheon the head cook at the Hôtel X would receive orders for several hundred dishes, all to be served at different times; he cooked few of them himself, but he gave instructions about all of them and inspected them before they were sent up. His memory was wonderful. The vouchers were pinned on a board, but the head cook seldom looked at them; everything was stored in his mind, and exactly to the minute, as each dish fell due, he would call out, 'Faites marcher une côtelette de veau' (or whatever it was) unfailingly. He was an insufferable bully, but he was also an artist. It is for their punctuality, and not for any superiority in technique, that men cooks are preferred to women.

The waiter's outlook is quite different. He too is proud in a way of his skill, but his skill is chiefly in being servile. His work gives him the mentality, not of a workman, but of a snob. He lives perpetually in sight of rich people, stands at their tables, listens to their conversation, sucks up to them with smiles and discreet little jokes. He has the pleasure of spending money by proxy. Moreover, there is always the chance that he may become rich himself, for, though most waiters die poor, they have long runs of luck occasionally. At some cafés on the Grand Boulevard there is so much money to be made that the waiters actually pay the patron for their employment. The result is that between constantly seeing money, and hoping to get it, the waiter comes to identify himself to some extent with his employers. He will take pains to serve a meal in style, because he feels that he is participating in the meal himself.

I remember Valenti telling me of some banquet at Nice at which he had once served, and of how it cost two hundred thousand francs and was talked of for months afterwards. 'It was splendid, mon p'tit, mais magnifique! Jesus Christ! The champagne, the silver, the orchids—I have never seen anything like them, and I have seen some things. Ah, it was glorious!'

'But,' I said, 'you were only there to wait?'

'Oh, of course. But still, it was splendid.'

The moral is, never be sorry for a waiter. Sometimes when you sit in a restaurant, still stuffing yourself half an hour after closing time, you feel that the tired waiter at your side must surely be despising you. But he is not. He is not thinking as he looks at you, 'What an overfed lout'; he is thinking, 'One day, when I have saved enough money, I shall be able to imitate that man.' He is ministering to a kind of pleasure he thoroughly understands and admires. And that is why waiters are seldom Socialists, have no effective trade union, and will work twelve hours a day—they work fifteen hours, seven days a week, in many cafés. They are snobs, and they find the servile nature of their work rather congenial.

The plongeurs, again, have a different outlook. Theirs is a job which offers no prospects, is intensely exhausting, and at the same time has not a trace of skill or interest; the sort of job that would always be done by women if women were strong enough. All that is required of them is to be constantly on the run, and to put up with long hours and a stuffy atmosphere. They have no way of escaping from this life, for they cannot save a penny from their wages, and working from sixty to a hundred hours a week leaves them no time to train for anything else. The best they can hope for is to find a slightly softer job as night watchman or lavatory attendant.

And yet the *plongeurs,* low as they are, also have a kind of pride. It is the pride of the drudge—the man who is equal to no matter what quantity of work. At that level, the mere power to go on working like an ox is about the only virtue attainable. *Débrouillard* is what every *plongeur* wants to be called. A *débrouillard* is a man who, even when he is told to do the impossible, will *se débrouiller*—get it done somehow. One of the kitchen *plongeurs* at the Hôtel X, a German, was well known as a *débrouillard*. One night an English lord came to the hotel, and the waiters were in despair, for the lord had asked for peaches, and there were none in stock; it was late at night, and the shops would be shut. 'Leave it to me,' said the German. He went out, and in ten minutes he was back with four peaches. He had gone into a neighbouring restaurant and stolen them. That is what is meant by a *débrouillard*. The English lord paid for the peaches at twenty francs each.

Mario, who was in charge of the *cafeterie*, had the typical drudge mentality. All he thought of was getting through the '*boulot,*' and he defied you to give him too much of it. Fourteen years underground had left him with about as much natural laziness as a piston rod. '*Faut être dur*', he used to say when anyone complained. You will often hear *plongeurs* boast, '*je suis dur*'—as though they were soldiers, not male charwomen.

Thus everyone in the hotel had his sense of honour, and when the press of work came we were all ready for a grand concerted effort to get through it. The constant war between the different departments also made for efficiency, for everyone clung to his own privileges and tried to stop the others idling and pilfering.

This is the good side of hotel work. In a hotel a huge and complicated machine is kept running by an inadequate staff, because every man has a well-defined job and does it scrupulously. But there is a weak point, and it is this—that the job the staff are doing is not necessarily what the customer pays for. The customer pays, as he sees it, for good service; the employee is paid, as he sees it, for the *boulot*—meaning, as a rule, an imitation of good service. The result is that, though hotels are miracles of punctuality, they are worse than the worst private houses in the things that matter.

Take cleanliness, for example. The dirt in the Hôtel

X, as soon as one penetrated into the service quarters, was revolting. Our *cafeterie* had year-old filth in all the dark corners, and the bread-bin was infested with cockroaches. Once I suggested killing these beasts to Mario. 'Why kill the poor animals?' he said reproachfully. The others laughed when I wanted to wash my hands before touching the butter. Yet we were clean where we recognized cleanliness as part of the *boulot*. We scrubbed the tables and polished the brass work regularly, because we had orders to do that; but we had no orders to be genuinely clean, and in any case we had no time for it. We were simply carrying out our duties; and as our first duty was punctuality, we saved time by being dirty.

In the kitchen the dirt was worse. It is not a figure of speech, it is a mere statement of fact to say that a French cook will spit in the soup—that is, if he is not going to drink it himself. He is an artist, but his art is not cleanliness. To a certain extent he is even dirty because he is an artist, for food, to look smart, needs dirty treatment. When a steak, for instance, is brought up for the head cook's inspection, he does not handle it with a fork. He picks it up in his fingers and slaps it down, runs his thumb round the dish and licks it to taste the gravy, runs it round and licks again, then steps back and contemplates the piece of meat like an artist judging a picture, then presses it lovingly into place with his fat, pink fingers, every one of which he has licked a hundred times that morning. When he is satisfied, he takes a cloth and wipes his fingerprints from the dish, and hands it to the waiter. And the waiter, of course, dips *his* fingers into the gravy—his nasty, greasy fingers which he is forever running through his brilliantined hair. When-ever one

pays more than, say, ten francs for a dish of meat in Paris, one may be certain that it has been fingered in this manner. In very cheap restaurants it is different; there, the same trouble is not taken over the food, and it is just forked out of the pan and flung on to a plate, without handling. Roughly speaking, the more one pays for food, the more sweat and spittle one is obliged to eat with it.

Dirtiness is inherent in hotels and restaurants, because sound food is sacrificed to punctuality and smartness. The hotel employee is too busy getting food ready to remember that it is meant to be eaten. A meal is simply 'une commande' to him, just as a man dying of cancer is simply 'a case' to the doctor. A customer orders, for example, a piece of toast. Somebody, pressed with work in a cellar deep underground, has to prepare it. How can he stop and say to himself, 'This toast is to be eaten—I must make it eatable'? All he knows is that it must look right and must be ready in three minutes. Some large drops of sweat fall from his forehead on to the toast. Why should he worry? Presently the toast falls among the filthy sawdust on the floor. Why trouble to make a new piece? It is much quicker to wipe the sawdust off. On the way upstairs the toast falls again, butter side down. Another wipe is all it needs. And so with everything. The only food at the Hôtel X which was ever prepared cleanly was the staff's, and the *patron*'s. The maxim, repeated by everyone, was: 'Look out for the *patron*, and as for the clients, *s'en f— pas mal!*' Everywhere in the service quarters dirt festered—a secret vein of dirt, running through the great garish hotel like the intestines through a man's body.

Apart from the dirt, the *patron* swindled the customers wholeheartedly. For the most part the materials of the food were very bad,

though the cooks knew how to serve it up in style. The meat was at best ordinary, and as to the vegetables, no good housekeeper would have looked at them in the market. The cream, by a standing order, was diluted with milk. The tea and coffee were of inferior sorts, and the jam was synthetic stuff out of vast, unlabelled tins. All the cheaper wines, according to Boris, were corked *vin ordinaire*. There was a rule that employees must pay for anything they spoiled, and in consequence damaged things were seldom thrown away. Once the waiter on the third floor dropped a roast chicken down the shaft of our service lift, where it fell into a litter of broken bread, torn paper, and so forth at the bottom. We simply wiped it with a cloth and sent it up again. Upstairs there were dirty tales of once-used sheets not being washed, but simply damped, ironed, and put back on the beds. The *patron* was as mean to us as to the customers. Throughout the vast hotel there was not, for instance, such a thing as a brush and pan; one had to manage with a broom and a piece of cardboard. And the staff lavatory was worthy of Central Asia, and there was no place to wash one's hands, except the sinks used for washing crockery.

In spite of all this the Hôtel X was one of the dozen most expensive hotels in Paris, and the customers paid startling prices. The ordinary charge for a night's lodging, not including breakfast, was two hundred francs. All wine and tobacco were sold at exactly double shop prices, though of course the *patron* bought at the wholesale price. If a customer had a title, or was reputed to be a millionaire, all his charges went up automatically. One morning, on the fourth floor, an American who was on diet wanted only salt and hot water for his breakfast. Valenti was furious. 'Jesus Christ!' he said, 'what about my ten per cent? Ten per cent of salt and water!' And he charged twenty-five francs for the breakfast. The customer paid without a murmur.

According to Boris, the same kind of thing went on in all Paris hotels, or at least in all the big, expensive ones. But I imagine that the customers at the Hôtel X were especially easy to swindle, for they were mostly Americans, with a sprinkling of English—no French—and seemed to know nothing whatever about good food. They would stuff themselves with disgusting American 'cereals,' and eat marmalade at tea, and drink vermouth after dinner, and order a *poulet à la reine* at a hundred francs and then souse it in Worcester sauce. One customer, from Pittsburg, dined every night in his bedroom on Grape-Nuts, scrambled eggs, and cocoa. Perhaps it hardly matters whether such people are swindled or not. **LP**

From Excellence to Superiority

Brooks Headley on why he left fine dining behind

Interview by Peter Meehan

Brooks Headley was the pastry chef at Del Posto—the four-star flagship of Mario Batali's Italianate flotilla—for seven years before decamping to a tiny tiled space in New York's East Village, where he opened Superiority Burger. Superiority is a vegetarian burger spot, the ideal place to take your kids for after-school gelato, and home of the best and most inventive vegetable-oriented cooking in the city at the moment. The food is cheap and all the serviceware is disposable, which led us to wonder, Why leave the ocean liner that is Del Posto for the dinghy that is Superiority Burger?

Were there things you wanted that SB has given you that a fine dining restaurant didn't?
Sure. I just wanted to sell good-quality food for cheap and have it be violently casual, friendly. No pretense of any kind other than us joking around with the people buying the food. It's quick, but we're not making fast food. Our food cost here is actually great, even using high-quality ingredients and selling them for cheap. But I have no beef with fancy restaurants at all. There are always going to be very fancy people who are going to want to go to places like that.

Are fancy places populated entirely by fancy people?
I'm guilty of saying, "Only rich people eat at fancy restaurants," which isn't

true. People who save up for a fancy occasion make up a big chunk, for sure. When I started at the first fancy place I worked, I'd never written HAPPY BIRTHDAY or HAPPY ANNIVERSARY in chocolate script. I'd say close to 50 percent of the desserts that went out had one or the other on them. Now I can write very well with chocolate, and I'll never have to do it again.

But while it isn't necessarily *all* hedge fund guys, fine dining *is* for very wealthy people and for normal people pretending to be rich for the night. Either way, a $400 meal for two is pretty grotesque. And the whole "we just want to pamper you and pretend to care about you while seething and hating you behind the scenes" service style is the worst.

There's a reason why everything at Superiority Burger is under ten bucks: it's completely accessible to whomever. That's a political statement—much more than the fact that we don't use any meat—because that's one of the things that always bummed me out about working in fancy restaurants: the cost. Honestly, I never cooked meat, because I was vegetarian for a long time, and then I was a pastry chef. I don't know how to butcher a goat, a cow, or a pig. The price here is the most important thing. Anyone can come in here and spend fifteen bucks and get three pretty well-thought-out farmers'-market side dishes.

We've figured out a way where I can go to the market and buy a bunch of ramps from Rick Bishop and a bunch of sunchokes from Franca Tantillo and asparagus from Stokes Farm, package that, and sell it for five bucks. I'm buying the same stuff as all the fancy restaurants in town. They're selling it within the context of a tasting menu or a $35 entrée. We're selling it in a little paper boat for $5.

How? What are the excessive costs in a fine dining situation? Tablecloths—
We have those things, too! We have a linen cost for uniforms. Fancy china only costs money once—we have to keep buying disposable containers!

If anything it's the portion size; none of our portions are huge. It's not an excessive, gross amount of food, but it's satisfying. Typically when people have complained about things being overpriced here, they're the people who come in and order one burger, eat it in three bites, and say, "That's it?" and don't get anything else. We're built to feed you a burger, one or two sides, and a dessert for under $20, and that's totally satisfying.

Why did you work in the fine dining restaurants you worked in instead of jumping ship earlier for something like this?
There's a certain regimen to working in a fine dining restaurant, and we've brought a lot of that here. We follow the same NYC Department of Health protocols—exactly to a T—that I followed at Del Posto. I would never have never understood cleanliness the way I do now if I had only worked at more casual restaurants.

I never planned to work in fine dining restaurants; I went with it because it was fun. I got psyched the more I did it. I could go to the market and buy four flats of the greatest peaches in Washington, D.C., make food with them, and serve it to people. That part has always been exciting, and I still get to do it.

At the fine dining restaurants where I worked, the food was always recognizable as what it was. I never worked at a place where the desserts were manipulated to the point that they were no longer a piece of fruit or a tart. You go to Le Bernardin and you get a piece of fish and sauce—a very cared-for, properly cooked piece of fish. That's what I want all the food to be like here. The main secret that makes the SB burger taste good is based on several cookbooks, things from fancy restaurants, and the techniques at Del Posto. I mixed it all in my head, and that's what makes the taste. When I look at other veggie burger recipes, it's not there.

Once we opened this place, all these places that sold veggie burgers popped up out of the blue. I don't think any of them knew about us or we knew about them; it just happened. But a lot of their burgers are not recognizable as food. They're highly processed, even if they're ethically sourced, vegan, organic, or fair trade.

Are fine dining restaurants necessary for that kind of transference of knowledge or are those the kind of lessons cooks are going to learn here, too?
The culture of cooks and sous chefs, especially in New York City, says that if you're serious and this is what you want to make a career out of, you *have* to work at Le Bernardin, Per Se, or Eleven Madison Park. I never worked at any of those places, but I worked at Del Posto and Campanile. And what I learned at those places informs how we cook here. That's not to say that you can only learn in fancy restaurants. A cook is going to learn from

whatever environment they're in. Julia, my sous chef, who is one of the greatest cooks that I've worked with, never worked in a fancy restaurant except for the six weeks I forced her to candy individual segments of grapefruit at Del Posto before she came here.

Stars, attention—that stuff was never interesting to you?
I think Michelin is the biggest crock of complete fucking bullshit—and please quote me exactly on this—especially in New York City. They lied about stuff they ate at Del Posto. But when you're in that world, it becomes something you strive for: lists and awards. It's part of the deal. Awards and lists are only really good for the second they're accepted, and then everything changes.

Now, I can walk around the East Village and there are lots of places that are open seven days a week that sell good-quality food for under twenty bucks. When I was a kid, I would visit New York for the food and record stores. In a way, I wanted this place to be like that. People can visit New York for fancy restaurants, but a twenty-year-old is not going to pop in to Le Bernardin. But they can come here and spend ten bucks on lunch and twenty on a record—it's more important for me to be part of *that* New York City. LP

From Stars to the Streets

Wes Avila on the choices a taquero makes

Interview by Gillian Ferguson

Wes Avila says he couldn't afford to work in fine dining. The LA native spent a year on the central California coast at L'Auberge Carmel, plating avocado mousse and poached lobster, before student loans sent him back to his hometown in search of a job that could pay his bills. Ultimately he found financial freedom while dodging the cops as an illegal taquero, selling beef-cheek tacos and sea-urchin-topped tostadas from a portable cart with GUERRILLA TACOS graffitied beneath the flat-top in lime-green spray paint. The name stuck, but the guerrilla lifestyle morphed into a legitimate taco truck with a Twitter handle and a schedule to keep. In a town crawling with *loncheras,* Avila's stands apart.

You have ingredients in your tacos that a lot of people would associate with fine dining, not taco trucks. That was kind of my thing. I wanted to make it approachable. When you hear foie gras, you're like, *Ooh fancy,* so I called it a fancy taco. I didn't sell it as a gimmick; I did it because I wanted to serve foie gras.

If I can get good urchin from someone in Santa Barbara who catches it the day before and brings it kicking and moving, then hell yeah I'm going to serve it. A lot of people haven't had it. My dad was like, *I haven't had it since I lived in Mexico.* You don't really see it in Mexican restaurants here, so when you do see it out of a truck and it's at a reasonable price, people order it. I try to take away that whole mystique.

There's this idea that tacos—really any food from a truck—are supposed to be cheap. Do you get a lot of pushback for selling $6 and $8 tacos?

We get more pushback from the truck than the cart. I had someone come one time and laugh like, *Haha, fucking $5 tacos?* And I was like, *Do you know where you're at, fool? This is LA, I know where I'm at.* He made me livid. I was like, *Do you see these ingredients?* And I pulled out the lobster and it was fucking moving. He ends up getting one and then ordering like five or six and then was all, *Yeah, this is the best lobster I've ever had.*

If you took those same ingredients off the tortilla and put them on a ceramic plate—

Yeah, I've done that demo for someone once. It was pork belly with a cherry salsa—cherries, pistachios, grilled red onion, vinegar, olive oil, habanero, and cilantro and a two- or three-ounce piece of seared pork belly from Krys Cook at Cook Pigs Ranch. And this guy was like, *Dude, this is five bucks? It's just pork.*

So I was like, *Bring me a plate.* They brought the plate out. I got my olive oil bottle out, made a swoosh, the whole thing, and was like, *Here: it's fucking $23.* And he said, *That's a good point, man—I'll take two.*

The fine dining opportunities for a cook in Los Angeles are few and far between. Would you recommend that a young cook in LA go have that experience?

I would tell them to go have that experience at least once. Honestly, other than the temples, I find it very, very difficult to see fine dining in the future. It's kind of cyclical—things go out of fashion and come back again. And I think right now fine dining isn't really in fashion. The food is the shit, the food is excellent, but you see more chefs going toward places like Bestia, Gjelina, where it's a little bit more rustic but really good quality.

What did fine dining do for you?

It opened my eyes to precision. There are places that are doing really good food, but it's so fast and rustic that you can't really see what the purity of ingredients can be. If you go to one of these temples—Providence or Mélisse—where they are really slowing it down and making beautiful, small, intricate food, it gives you a different perspective on things. There is obviously a lot of work that goes into it—and a lot of guys working for free—so you can see the hands that go into the food, you know what I mean? I'm really, really grateful that I did that and took that route of fine dining, because it taught me about discipline and preserving ingredients and getting the best stuff. And stamina—you're working twelve hours, you know?

Is there anything you miss about that temple environment?

No. There's nothing I miss about it even though it's a beautiful thing. Certain cooks aspire for perfection, but you'll kill yourself trying to make it, and you'll kill yourself trying to keep it. If it's worth it to you, follow it. But if you're not going to be the chef at one of those places, and you actually want to make a living, there's no way you can do it there.

My endgame isn't Michelin stars, it's to do really well with tacos, make something scalable, sell everything, and move to Hawaii and open a small taco shack that I can open three days a week and sell local fish tacos and have my own hours. It's not about making tons of money and having a mansion. I still want to be able to work, but I want to do it at my pace. When I started Guerrilla Tacos, that was the beauty of it: *Fuck it, let's open today!* Now we have to be on time and do this and that. But that's what I liked about it before, so I think I'd revert to that and be financially free. **LP**

UNCAGE ASIA'S BEER

   @TIGERBEERUS

ENJOY RESPONSIBLY
www.TIGERBEERUS.com

GOURMET DINNER

$for 1^{99}$

OR LESS!

by Tamara Shopsin + Jason Fulford

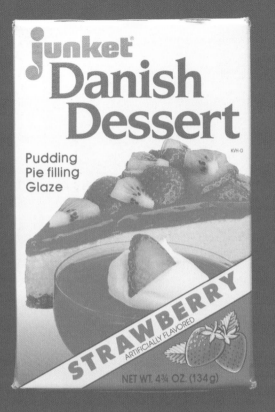

junket®
Danish
Dessert

Pudding
Pie filling
Glaze

KVH-0

STRAWBERRY
ARTIFICIALLY FLAVORED

NET WT. 4¾ OZ. (134g)

KEN'S
STEAK HOUSE
Russian
Dressing

Wish·Bone
THE
BOLDER
THE
BETTER
Deluxe
French
Great on
Sandwiches!
Flavor you can see!

Bell·View
HOT CHOPPED
HOAGIE SPREAD
16 FL OZ (1 PT) 473mL

WITH
NATURAL
SPICES
• No MSG†
• No Artificial
  Flavors
McCormick
Au Jus Gravy
MIX
NET WT. 1 OZ (28g)

Redner's
WAREHOUSE MARKETS
Serving Our Local Communities Since 1970
PREMIUM
DECAF
GROUND COFFEE
MEDIUM ROAST
MEDIUM
BALANCED
FLAVOR
FOR ALL COFFEE MAKERS

Fancy Chicken

BY SAM HENDERSON

For this edition of Three Dishes, we asked Sam Henderson, the former chef de cuisine of wd~50 in New York, about her approach to chicken—the possibilities of the bird and the ways she likes to cook it.

When I think about cooking chicken in restaurants, I think of two extremes: 1) throwing it in the pressure fryer at Chick-fil-A, which was my first kitchen job—in a mall, no less—and 2) how I learned to cook chicken from Wylie Dufresne. In a fine dining restaurant, chicken doesn't really go on the menu unless you can do something super weird or super delicious with it. And in my experience at wd~50, chicken was usually super weird *and* super delicious, like the "chicken ball" that Mike Sheerin used to make: boned-out chicken contorted and meat-glued together into a softball of meat, covered in a layer of skin, deep-fried, and served with mole (that had been turned into a sheet of paper) and egg yolk (that had the texture of American cheese).

Chicken is the friendliest protein, open to a world of possibilities: you can turn it into something that doesn't even remotely resemble chicken, or you can throw it in the oven whole and know it'll come out good. You can turn it into sausage; you can fry it in your backyard; you can throw it in a smoker; you can use the feet and the back and make a really great stock.

If I'm cooking at home, I'm going to make something like the whole roast bird here: a great reward for very little work. The Hawaiian chicken came about as sort of a joke—an intentionally ridiculous but still delicious dish that I first made for staff meal at wd~50. The chicken sausage with broccoli hash is the sort of dish that you might see on a fine dining menu, yet it can be replicated at home. To me they represent three modes of chicken cookery: one that makes you feel comforted, one that makes you smile, and one that might make you cock your head a little and wonder, *What's that?* All are delicious.

Roast Chicken

Whole roast chicken with soy-agave glaze

One night, I was roasting eggplant, and I had this concoction of soy sauce, spices, and agave lying around—so I put some on the bird we were roasting, too. I decided that I liked it more on the chicken than on the eggplant, and it became my go-to chicken glaze. I've tried a bunch of different glazes and bastes over time—I really like a combination of honey, butter, and *berbere* spice, too—but this is my favorite. It's a little sweet, there's some umami from the soy sauce, and there's a little bit of fragrance from the coriander.

There's not a whole lot more trickery to the dish. There's a little bit of seasoned schmaltz under the skin, to season and baste the breast meat. It's stuffed with lemon, thyme, and garlic, which add a really nice aroma as it cooks. And I roast the chicken on a rack, not because it gets the skin super crispy or helps it cook evenly, but because it makes it easy to move the cooked bird, to collect all the juices from the pan, and to clean up afterwards. Ease should not be underrated, especially on a weeknight.

MAKES 4 SERVINGS

INGREDIENTS

¼ **C** schmaltz (Empire Kosher brand schmaltz is good if you don't have any hiding in your freezer)

+ kosher salt

+ freshly ground black pepper

1 bunch thyme

1 fresh bay leaf

1 whole chicken (4–5 lbs)

1 head garlic, one clove grated and the rest of the head halved

1 lemon, halved

+ butcher's twine, for trussing

+ olive oil, for greasing

2 T soy sauce

⅓ **C** agave

½ **t** ground coriander

1 T all-purpose flour

¼ **C** milk

6 T chicken stock or water

1. Season the schmaltz: In a small pot, steep the schmaltz, a pinch of salt, a few turns of black pepper, 2 sprigs of thyme, and the bay leaf over very low heat for 2 hours. Chill until firm.

2. Heat the oven to 350°F. Stuff the chicken with the halved garlic head, the lemon, and the rest of the thyme. Tuck the wings behind the back, cross the legs, and truss. Gently lift the skin around the breast and stuff with the seasoned schmaltz. Season the whole bird with salt and pepper and place on a greased oven rack set over a rimmed baking sheet. Leave out at room temperature for 1 hour, then place in the oven.

3. Make the glaze: Whisk together the soy sauce, agave, coriander, and grated garlic in a small bowl. Reserve 2 tablespoons.

4. As the chicken roasts, baste with the glaze and pan drippings every 20 minutes. Rotate the bird halfway through cooking. Cook until the leg reads 155°F or the juices run clear, about 90 minutes. Let rest at least 15 minutes.

5. While the chicken rests, add 1 tablespoon of the pan drippings to a small saucepan. Whisk in the flour to form a roux, then whisk in the milk, chicken stock, and the reserved 2 tablespoons of glaze. Keep whisking over low heat for 10 minutes. Season with pepper.

6. Carve the bird into breasts, wings, thighs, drumsticks, and butt (the best!). Sauce and serve.

Fried Chicken

Hawaiian chicken with Spam fried rice

We always had great staff meals at wd~50; they were a very important part of everyone's day. Everybody had their go-tos. I would normally make homey family meals, like roast pork or chili or chicken and dumplings. One day I felt like breaking up the routine and doing something silly, because every so often it's nice to put together a staff meal that makes everybody giggle a little bit. We happened to have all of the things on hand that you would need to make something inauthentically Hawaiian. We had pineapples, we always had chicken around, and I stole some cherries from the bar. I don't know why we had Spam—I may have actually purchased the Spam to round out the dish. Anyway, it was the start of this dish making semi-regular appearances in staff-meal situations and beyond.

MAKES 4 SERVINGS

INGREDIENTS

6 T white vinegar

2 T mirin

1 C + 2 T soy sauce

1 1" piece ginger, peeled and julienned

2 lbs boneless, skinless chicken thighs, cut into 1–1½" pieces

1 T sugar

1 C all-purpose flour

2 eggs, lightly beaten

2 C ground cornflakes, seasoned with kosher salt and freshly ground black pepper

1 C chicken stock

½ t *sansho* pepper

½ C brown sugar, tightly packed

2 6-oz cans pineapple juice, reduced by half

1 piece star anise

2 t cornstarch

5 drops red food coloring

+ canola oil, for frying

1 small carrot, julienned

1 scallion, greens only, julienned and held in ice water

¼ pineapple, cut into ½" pieces

+ Spam Fried Rice

10 maraschino cherries with stems

1. Pickle the ginger: Stir the white vinegar, mirin, and ¼ cup of the soy sauce together in a bowl. Add the ginger and allow to marinate for at least 10 minutes, though longer is better—up to 24 hours. Set aside.

2. Bread the chicken: Place the chicken in a large mixing bowl with the sugar and 2½ tablespoons of soy sauce. Massage until evenly coated. Add the flour, beaten eggs, and cornflakes to three separate bowls, and set a rack over a rimmed baking sheet. Keeping one hand dry, dredge the pieces of chicken in flour, then the egg, and then place on the rack. Once all of the chicken pieces have been egg-washed and "drip-dried," dredge them in the cornflake mix. Check to make certain all the pieces have an even breading. Place on a new baking sheet and refrigerate.

3. Make the glaze: In a medium saucepan over medium heat, bring the remaining soy sauce, chicken stock, sansho pepper, brown sugar, pineapple juice, and star anise to a simmer. Simmer for 5 minutes, then remove the star anise. Mix the cornstarch in a small bowl with a small amount of glaze, then whisk back into the rest of the glaze. Bring to a boil and cook for 1 more minute. Stir in the food coloring and keep warm until ready to use.

4. Fill a large, deep pot with 4–5 inches of canola oil and heat to 350°F. Fry the chicken in batches until it reaches a deep golden brown and is cooked through, about 3–5 minutes. Toss the chicken and glaze in a mixing bowl to coat. Add the carrot, scallion, pineapple, and pickled ginger, and toss once more. Place over **Spam Fried Rice**, garnish with maraschino cherries, and serve family-style.

SPAM FRIED RICE

1 T unsalted butter

1 C jasmine rice

2 cloves garlic, smashed

1 t turmeric

½ t cumin

1 piece star anise

+ kosher salt, to taste

2 C water

1 T coconut oil

½ yellow onion, diced

½ can Spam, cut into a large dice (about ¼ cup)

1. In a large skillet over medium heat, melt the butter and add the rice. Toast the rice, stirring until it takes on a light golden-brown hue and the smell hits you in the face. Add the garlic, turmeric, cumin, star anise, salt, and water, and stir to combine. Bring to a simmer and cover. Cook over low heat until the rice is cooked through, about 20–30 minutes. Discard the star anise, remove the rice from the pan, and spread out on a baking sheet to dry for several hours. (You can also use any leftover rice you have lying around.)

2. Melt the coconut oil in a large sauté pan over high heat and add half of the diced onion. Cook, stirring, until caramelized, about 5 minutes. Add half of the Spam and cook, stirring, until browned, another 2 minutes. Add half of the cooked rice, toss a few times, and season with salt to taste. Plate on a serving platter. Repeat with remaining onion, rice, and Spam, and serve.

Chicken Sausage

Boudin blanc with mustard, potato noodles, and broccoli crumbs

I came up with the recipe for this sausage when we put a version of cassoulet on the menu at wd-50. Sausage was something I learned how to make in Chicago, when I was working at the Publican; I like the transformative nature of the process as well as, you know, eating good sausage.

Sausage and pasta can be great together, or they can be like cafeteria food. Here, I've substituted "noodles" made from potatoes that have been rinsed of their starch and sautéed over high heat, so they still have quite a bit of crunch to them. I think the potato-y flavor knocks you over the head a little bit, which is not really something people normally say about potatoes. My friend and former colleague Simone Tong introduced me to potatoes cooked this way, but hers were seasoned very differently—they were spicy Sichuan-style potato threads.

Mustard and sausage go well together, so I concocted a mustardy sauce. But the dish needed some crunch. I combined broccoli, garlic, and lemon to make a *gremolata,* and I threw it in the oven overnight. It gives you this really nice crunchy crumb that's great to throw on pasta or fish or salad, too. So the potatoes are Sichuan style, the sausage is French, and the broccoli hash is my own weird invention—my hope is that it all hits you with the same satisfaction as eating a hot dog.

MAKES 4 SERVINGS

INGREDIENTS

2 heads broccoli, florets only

2 t olive oil

2 cloves garlic, Microplaned

1 lemon, zest Microplaned and juice reserved

¼ t crushed red pepper

+ kosher salt

2 Idaho potatoes, julienned lengthwise

1 C heavy cream

4 thyme sprigs

2 T Dijon mustard

+ neutral oil

4 Boudin Blanc Sausages

+ freshly ground black pepper

+ white pepper

1. Make the broccoli crumbs: Heat the oven to 170°F. Pulse the broccoli, olive oil, garlic, lemon zest, red pepper flakes, and a pinch of salt in a food processor until finely chopped and completely combined. Spread on a rimmed baking sheet in a single layer and dry in the oven for 3–4 hours (or in a low dehydrator overnight). When done, the broccoli should be crunchy and look like weed.

2. Rinse the julienned potatoes thoroughly in cold water, then place them in a bowl of cold, lightly salted water for another 15 minutes, or until ready to use.

3. Meanwhile, make the mustard sauce: Heat the cream and thyme in a small saucepan over medium heat. Simmer, uncovered, until reduced by half, about 5 minutes. Remove the thyme, then stir in the mustard. Keep warm.

4. Heat the oven to 300°F.

5. Heat a cast-iron skillet over medium heat and coat the bottom with neutral oil. Sear the **Boudin Blanc** until brown on all sides, about 2 minutes. Finish warming the sausages through in the oven for about 3–4 minutes.

6. While the sausages cook, remove the potato noodles from the water with a spider or slotted spoon and place in a strainer to dry. (It's important not to dump everything through the strainer; you want to get rid of the starch at the bottom of the bowl). Heat a large skillet and coat with a tablespoon of neutral oil. Sauté the potato noodles in batches, tossing until cooked but still crunchy, about 3 minutes. Season with salt and black pepper, and plate.

7. Season the warm mustard sauce with salt, white pepper, and reserved lemon juice. (If the sauce is too thick, you can loosen it with a bit of water.) Slice the sausage into rounds and place on top of the potato noodles. Drizzle each plate with 2 spoonfuls of mustard sauce and garnish with broccoli hash.

BOUDIN BLANC

The key to perfectly seasoned sausage is working with ingredients by weight, not volume. Break out the gram scale!

1 hank sheep casings

455 g chicken breast, cubed

170 g thick-cut bacon, cut into lardons

56 g fatback, cubed

2 g kosher salt

5 g Instacure #1

1 g toasted fennel seeds

2 g Colman's dry mustard powder

2 g onion powder

2 g garlic powder

5 g ground coriander

1 g white pepper

110 g ice water

40 g nonfat powdered milk

Special equipment: sausage stuffer, meat grinder (with small die; about 3/16"), stand mixer, and paddle attachment. Temperature is crucial! Keep all ingredients/equipment very cold.

1. Make the farce: Rinse the sheep casings in cold water, and keep them in a bowl of cold water in the refrigerator. Combine the chicken breast, bacon, fatback, salt, Instacure #1, and spices in a large mixing bowl and mix with your hands to incorporate. Place in the freezer for at least 1 hour to par-freeze, along with the grinder attachments and sausage stuffer. Temper the stand-mixer bowl by filling it with ice water; place the paddle attachment inside.

2. After the meats have par-frozen, run them through the grinder two times. Empty the mixer bowl, and dry. Move the ground meats to the mixer bowl, add the ice water, and mix with the paddle attachment, gradually increasing the speed. Once the meat looks emulsified (after approximately 5 minutes), and when you hear it wicking off the sides of the bowl, stop the mixer. Add the powdered milk, scrape down the sides of the bowl, and turn the mixer back on, bringing up to top speed for about 1 minute. Stop and cook off a small patty to taste for seasoning. It should be well seasoned and should not look greasy. (If it appears greasy, the sausage is not emulsified.)

3. Stuff the sausage: Place the farce in the cold sausage stuffer, with the medium funnel attached.

Pull the casings out of the water (it's important to keep them damp to prevent tearing) and wrap them around the funnel, leaving one funnel length's worth of slack. Tie off the end of the casing and proceed to stuff. Once all of the farce is spent, tie off the sausage and make your links: twist the sausage in alternate directions every 5–6 inches. Refrigerate overnight.

4. Cook the sausage: Bring a pot of water up to 160°F. Place the sausages in water for approximately 10–20 minutes, or until they reach an internal temperature of 147°F. Shock in ice water and hold in the refrigerator until ready to use. **LP**

Contrib

Sascha Bos is a freelance writer whose work has appeared in *Render*, *LA Weekly*, and *East Bay Express*. She has edited titles including *Little Flower Baking*, *Das Cookbook*, and *Drink: Los Angeles* and spent a year researching nineteenth-century cookbooks and feminism for her UC Berkeley honors thesis. She wants to work for you.

Jose Miguel Méndez Cristina is a Spanish illustrator based in London, with an artistic background in graphic design and moving images. Drawing inspiration from underground comics and skateboarding culture, he explores humorous and sometimes unsettling themes using strong colors and typography with an emphasis on character design.

Pablo Delcan is a designer, animator, and illustrator from Spain, and the founder of Delcan & Company. His work has been awarded and recognized by the Type Directors Club, Art Directors Club, and the *New York Times*.

Gillian Ferguson is a writer and radio producer. She lives in Los Angeles, where she eats *tlayudas* once a week.

Born in Metro Detroit, Lyndon French is an artist who lives and works out of Chicago, IL. Aside from creating images, he enjoys romantic joyrides in his Astro van, accompanied by a cup of vanilla-bean ice cream. For a taller male, he's quite elegant on a pair of roller skates.

Jason Fulford is a photographer and co-founder of J&L Books. He is a Guggenheim Fellow and a contributing editor to *Blind Spot*. He is a frequent lecturer at universities, and has led workshops across the United States and in Japan, Italy, Poland, the Netherlands, Germany, and Spain. His monographs include *Sunbird* (Bird Entertainment, 2000), *Crushed* (J&L Books, 2003), *Raising Frogs for $$$* (The Ice Plant, 2006), *The Mushroom Collector* (The Soon Institute, 2010), and *Hotel Oracle* (The Soon Institute, 2013). He is co-author with Tamara Shopsin of the children's photo book *This Equals That* (Aperture, 2014), and co-editor with Gregory Halpern of *The Photographer's Playbook* (Aperture, 2014).

Walter Green is a graphic designer based in San Francisco, CA.

Clay Hickson is a freelance illustrator living in Chicago, IL. His work is a hodgepodge of influences ranging from 1960s underground ephemera to West Coast airbrush illustration, with a little splash of Northern California–New Age–hippie aesthetic.

Tienlon Ho is a writer based in San Francisco, CA. *Merci beaucoup*, Constance d'Ornellas-Chancerelle, for her help speaking the language of nouvelle cuisine. Read more at *tienlon.com*.

Alex Jenkins is an illustrator and cartoonist from (and stuck in) the suburbs of South London. He graduated from Camberwell College of Arts in 2015 with a B.A. in illustration.

Aleksandra Kingo is a London-based photographer from Vilnius, Lithuania. With her fashion and still-life photography, she walks the razor's edge between discomfort and sexiness, toying with viewers' senses of disgust and attraction and creating quirky worlds where lipstick stains are a blessing and bananas are pastel-pink. She gains a lot of inspiration from everyday life stories as well as popular and Internet culture.

Bourree Lam writes about economics at *The Atlantic*. She is an XO-sauce connoisseur and milk-tea enthusiast.

utors

Karen Leibovitz is a writer and a restaurant person whose most recent project is The Perennial, an environmentally sustainable restaurant and bar in SF where she is co-founder with her husband, Anthony Myint. She's also a partner in Mission Chinese Food and Commonwealth and co-author of *Atelier Crenn: The Metamorphosis of Taste* and *Mission Street Food: Recipes and Ideas from an Improbable Restaurant*.

John Lisle is a Brooklyn-based illustrator concentrating in work representing abstract and human forms, as well as everything in between. His favorite emoji is the chipmunk.

Jaci Kessler Lubliner is an illustrator, art director, and future mom.

Jim Meehan, a bar operator, educator, and author of *The PDT Cocktail Book*, worked at some of New York City's most popular restaurants and bars, including Gramercy Tavern and the Pegu Club, before opening the James Beard Award–winning bar PDT in 2007. The former editor of *Food & Wine* magazine's annual cocktail book and the *Mr. Boston Bartender's Guide*, Meehan currently serves

as the drinks editor for *Tasting Table*, the global ambassador for Banks Rums, and the curator of the cocktail programs for American Express Centurion lounges nationally.

Paige Mehrer is an illustrator living in Brooklyn who recently graduated from the Rhode Island School of Design. Follow her work at *paigemehrer.com* or on Instagram @paigemehrer.

Christine Muhlke is the editor-at-large for *Bon Appétit* and the founder of Bureau X consultancy. She has co-authored books with David Kinch, Eric Ripert, and Eric Werner.

Corey Olsen is a photographer from Maine, currently based in Brooklyn, NY. He received his BFA from the School of Visual Arts in 2014. His work has been exhibited internationally and nationally, most recently at Julie Saul Gallery in New York, following his first monograph, *Garage Still Lifes*, with Silent Sound Books.

Kevin Pang is a writer and filmmaker in Chicago, IL.

Tamara Shopsin is a graphic designer and illustrator whose work is regularly

featured in the *New York Times* and the *New Yorker*. She is the author of the memoir *Mumbai New York Scranton*, designer of the *5 Year Diary*, and creator of the children's book *What Is This?*. She is also a cook at her family's restaurant, Shopsin's, in New York.

Alex Toledano lives in and likes to think about Paris. He received his Ph.D. in History at UC Berkeley and is the president of VISTO Images, an art consultancy.

Lucas Turner is a cook and musician living in the Bay Area and currently working on a live-action adaptation of *Aladdin* with *Lucky Peach*'s San Francisco office.

Armando Veve is an illustrator who lives and works in Philadelphia, PA.

Eric Wolfinger is a photographer who shoots from the heart and goes for the gut. Passionate and purpose-driven, he works on projects that move the needle toward the greater good. After a dozen award-winning books and hundreds of commissions, he has the reputation of a close collaborator whose immersive approach results in powerful storytelling.

SIGHTS N' SNACKS

MEXICO CITY

by T. Shopsin

EJECUTIVO ON THE WAY TO EAT AT PUJOL

SQUASH-BLOSSOM QUESADILLA (SIN QUESO)

TP DISPENSER AT MUSEO DEL OBJETO DEL OBJETO

PAPA SMURF COOKIE

HOMEMADE TOYS AT FRIDA KAHLO'S CASA AZUL

BIKE STORE THAT WAS CLOSED

JAPANESE TOURIST WITH A NECK TATTOO

FRESHLY CUT CHURROS

JELL-O SHAPED LIKE DEVO HATS

WAITRESS AT A SANBORNS CAFETERIA